IN SEARCH OF

Motif No. 1

IN SEARCH OF

Motif No. 1

· ·

THE HISTORY *of a* FISH SHACK

L.M. VINCENT

Charleston · London

THE
History
PRESS

Published by The History Press
Charleston, SC 29403
www.historypress.net

Front cover: The Motif, by Ken Knowles (b. 1968). Oil on canvas [24 x 20 in.].
Courtesy of Pat Lambert.
Back cover: top left: © copyright 2011 Robert M. Ring; *top right*: courtesy of the Sandy Bay
Historical Society; *bottom*: courtesy of Mary Faino.

First published 2011

Manufactured in the United States

ISBN 978.1.60949.382.0

Vincent, Lawrence M.
In search of Motif No. 1 : the history of a fish shack / L.M. Vincent.
p. cm.
Includes bibliographical references.
ISBN 978-1-60949-382-0
1. Motif No. 1 (Rockport, Mass. : Building) 2. Historic buildings--Massachusetts--
Rockport. 3. Fishing huts--Massachusetts--Rockport. 4. Artists--Massachusetts--Rockport.
5. Historic buildings in art. 6. Rockport (Mass.)--Buildings, structures, etc. 7. Rockport
(Mass.)--History. 8. Rockport (Mass.)--Intellectual life. I. Title.
F74.R68V56 2011
974.1'53--dc23
2011036867

Dedicated to the people of Rockport—past, present and future —especially the artists.

CONTENTS

Acknowledgements

L egions of people contributed in innumerable ways to this book, but Cynthia Peckham, Erik A.R. Ronnberg Jr. and John D. Buckley were indispensable. Simply, this book could not have been written without them.

Buddy Woods, Bill Donovan, Don Atkinson and Captain Bill Lee also played critical roles in plugging historical gaps that no written sources could ever fill.

Rockport artist Arnold Knauth, a living link to the glory days of the Rockport art colony, brought to life the artists whom I had only known through paintings or by reading about them. A number of other Cape Ann artists were instrumental in my understanding and appreciation of the artwork so central to this story, and I delighted in the time spent with them. They include Don Mosher, Tom Nicholas, Ken Knowles, Bernie Gerstner, Ron Straka, Dorothy J. Ramsey Stoffa, David Tutwiler, Liné Tutwiler, Wil Mackay, Jeff Weaver, Isabel Natti, the late Ann Fiske and the late Mary Robins-Murphy.

Gallery owners and collectors shared their passion for Cape Ann art with me, allowing me access to their collections and, in many cases, generously providing or arranging for the wonderful paintings reproduced in these pages. I am particularly indebted to Daniel R. McDougall of McDougall Fine Arts, Gloucester; Stuart Pocock of Pocock Fine Arts, Fort Lauderdale, Florida; Tom Davies; Joel Berenson, MD; and William Trayes. Others who aided in this regard include Ellery H. Kurtz of Godel Fine Arts, New York City; Abbot W. Vose and Robert C. Vose III of the Vose Galleries, Boston; Roger Armstrong of State of the Art Galleries, Gloucester; Leon Lowe of Thistle Fine Art, Rockport; David B. Cox of Main Street Art and Antiques,

Gloucester; and Wilbur James. I am also grateful for the enthusiastic cooperation of the Rockport Art Association, with special thanks to Carol Linsky and Linda Cote. The private collectors who have provided me with reproductions of works from their collections but have remained anonymous deserve special thanks as well.

Others who contributed to my obtaining images and/or permission to reproduce them include Jim Orr and Stephanie Lucas of the Henry Ford Museum, Dearborn, Michigan; Ila Furman of the Corcoran Gallery of Art, Washington, D.C.; Jonathan Notling of the Cincinnati Art Museum; Kajette Bloomfield of Bridgeman Art Library International; and Peter Anderson and Sandra Corrao of the Rockport National Bank. Robert M. Ring and Linda A. Marquette have my gratitude for photographic services. Fred Buck of the Cape Ann Museum assumed the mantle of coordinator extraordinaire for nearly all of the images; I continually relied on him to work his digital magic, and he never let me down. The editing equivalent of Fred was my daughter Caitlin, who provided first-class professional services at the family rate.

For helping me navigate their collections and holdings, I particularly want to thank Stephanie Buck at the Cape Ann Museum and Gwen Stephenson of the Sandy Bay Historical Society. I also want to recognize Linda Johnson and Martha Oaks of the Cape Ann Museum, Paul Dobbs of the Massachusetts College of Art and Design, Judy Oski of the Gloucester Lyceum and Sawyer Free Library, Laura Smith of the George Eastman Archive and Study Center and staff members at the Boston Public Library, the Gloucester Archives, the Essex County Registry of Deeds, the Phillips Library of the Peabody Essex Museum, Widener Library of Harvard University, the Beebe Communications Library of Boston University and the Archives of American Art at the Smithsonian Institution.

Present and past town of Rockport officials and employees who aided and abetted this project include John Tomasz, George Robertson, Jack Monroe, Frederick Frithsen, Patricia Brown, Diane Lashua, Nick Barletta, Rosemary Lesch and Roger Lesch. The following either provided specific guidance or assistance or rounded out the story in often essential, and sometimes unexpected, ways: Leslie Bartlett, Mitchell Bradley, Allan Brandt, Alvin Brown III, the late Donald Buckley, Lonnie Busch, Elaine Hibbard Clark, Judith Curtis, James Craig, William Flynn, Peter Hope, the late Joseph Garland, Malcolm J. Hibbard, George Hobbs, Ray Lamont, George (Nick) Mackay, Jack Medoff, Joe Mitchell, the late Eleanor Parsons, Richard Pollay, Karen Quinn, Jay Smith, Mark Stolle, Larry Story, Debbie Waddell, James Waddell, Lyn Watson and Peter Weber.

Professor James Conron of Clark University schooled me on the picturesque and regionalism in American art. Lisa Harrington and Brian Powell at Building Conservation Associates valiantly attempted to decipher paint history from weathered wood scraps. Dr. Carol Benson provided me work schedule flexibility, without which I never would have met deadline.

Being able to pick up the phone and call friends like Keith Raffel, Robert A. Adams, Charles Porter, Robert N. Reeves III, Mark Shwayder and David White for advice and morale boosting made my work easier, as did the ever-present support of my sister Jan and my wife and daughters. I am also grateful to the folks at The History Press, most notably my commissioning editor, Jeff Saraceno, for taking on a somewhat quirky project and indulging its author.

Finally, I honor the memory of my late cousin Al Cohen of Peabody, Massachusetts, who started things off by recommending I visit Rockport to see Motif No. 1 for the first time. Most importantly, when I repeatedly asked, "What is Motif No. 1?" he refused to tell me.

"You'll see," he said with his mischievous smile.

And I did.

Chapter 1
ENTER Motif No. 1

In Which the Narrator and the Fish Shack Are Introduced

I was well past spring chicken–hood by the time I first laid eyes on Motif No.1. It was a cool and clear October morning, and the town of Rockport, Massachusetts, roughly forty miles northeast of Boston on the coast of Cape Ann, was quiet. From T-Wharf—the appropriately alphabetically configured pier extending from the mouth of Rockport Harbor—I gazed in silent homage at the small barn-like structure at the end of the adjacent stone pier.

Acutely aware of the importance of this first impression, I patiently awaited a flood of transformative sensations: responses to not just the tableau before me but to the aura of the surrounding town and harbor. Before me was a structure of great interest, a famous and historic place. Should I be feeling elation? A sense of the sublime? A connection with a glorious, fascinating and heroic past?

Motif No.1 didn't fit into the mold of any important tourist site I'd experienced. The shack is neither a marvel of engineering nor a true historic site in the sense of Monticello or Mount Vernon. It's not famous through association with a Revolutionary or Civil War battle, no one notable ever slept in it, no literary masterpieces were associated with it and no acclaimed architect designed it. But quaint and picturesque? For sure.

I strained, without success, for something more profound. As I stood, a tourist on a wharf, I wasn't exactly sure how I felt, other than confused.

In fairness, I was at a distinct disadvantage at this first meeting with the Motif. I have never been closely associated with the sea, unlike most writers who broach these subjects. Not that I personally know any maritime authors, but I definitely admire their photographs on book jackets: at the helm of a sailboat in waterproof gear, tanned and leathery-looking, hair windblown, an adventuresome smile. Opening those books, one can almost smell the salt air and imagine the pages rustling from a prevailing northeasterly breeze. These are writers who brave dangerous waters, challenge the great forces of nature, wear Old Spice and know how to tie a whole bunch of knots.

In contrast, I come from Kansas. I have never caught a fish and didn't see a live lobster until age twelve at the Colony Steak House in Kansas City—a very nice restaurant, as I recollect, and likely the only one in town with a live lobster tank instead of frozen tails from South Africa. They were piled upon one another in the corner of the tank as if they had just completed a short-yardage running play in a game of crustacean football. At the time, I was stunned that the ugly critters weren't red like in the cartoons.

Although I have been on sailboats a handful of times, these excursions have not been without trepidation—not fear of drowning but, rather, the anxiety that I will be assigned tasks that involve ropes. Once, when sailing in Long Island Sound with a college roommate, when my utter lack of nautical cognition resulted in a capsize, my otherwise good-natured friend called me an idiot with such sincerity and conviction that the memory still stings after forty years.

But back at T-Wharf and not knowing quite what to do, I did what hundreds of thousands—perhaps millions—of people have done in my situation. I pulled out my camera and took a picture. (Plate 1)

It's a pretty bare-bones snapshot of Motif No. 1, except for the antique lobster buoys bolted to its side (so tourists can't swipe them). There are no picturesque boats alongside and no picturesque lobstermen toiling away. Even the sparse, wispy clouds are singularly undramatic and bland.

But one shouldn't be deceived by this candid snapshot of a glamour queen caught without her make-up. This is no simple fish shack; it is a celebrity—and no flash-in-the-pan celebrity either but an institution, the heart and soul of an entire community and one of the most recognizable structures in the country (and some might argue the world). While seemingly unpretentious and unaffected, Motif No. 1 is famous, and fame is undeniably intimidating in any incarnation.

Consider. Its countenance graces innumerable refrigerator magnets, postcards, art photographs, giclée prints, Christmas cards, calendars, place mats, shot glasses, T-shirts, souvenir spoons and faux scrimshaw cribbage boards. A perfume was named after it. It has its own Sebastian miniature model and its own transfer ware plates by Staffordshire, in both red and blue. The Motif has graced the pages of *Life*, *Look* and *Yankee* magazines, has made legitimate headlines in the *New York Times*, *Time* and other newspapers and newsweeklies and is referenced in the *American Art Review* and scholarly art publications. Its visage hangs in Rockport public buildings like a presidential portrait, and Rockport postal workers proudly sport a tiny Motif No. 1 embroidered on their shirts and blouses. It greets visitors on the sign entering town and has its own special "Motif No. 1 Day" in Rockport. For Pete's sake, it even has its own U.S. thirty-four-cent postage stamp.

But we haven't even scratched the surface until we come to the Motif's artistic accomplishments and credentials, its *raison d'être*, if you will. It has been sketched, etched, block-printed, watercolored, acryliced and oiled by countless well-known, not-so-well-known and totally unknown artists and artist wannabes. It hangs on the walls of major art museums, prestigious galleries and elite private collections. Significant works of art bear no more than its name for a title. To the Rockport Colony of artists past and present, the Motif represents what Rouen Cathedral was to Monet, what Madame X was to Sargent, what Helga was to Wyeth and what Elizabeth Siddal was to Dante Gabriel Rossetti (here I must confess that I took some art history courses in college but never used them until now).

This, in short, is the Mother of All Fish Shacks.

All of which probably accounts for my being rather perplexed, as I've confessed, standing on the end of T-Wharf on that pleasant October day.

Because I didn't know any of this.

To put it bluntly, I'd never heard of Motif No.1 before that day. Not ever.

IN WHICH THE NARRATOR REASSURES OTHERS WHO ALSO HAVE NEVER HEARD OF MOTIF NO. 1

Later that day, as I wandered through the shops on Bearskin Neck, idly examining a Motif No. 1 sewing thimble, I tried to convince myself that the shack did look vaguely familiar. I had seen pictures of it somewhere, perhaps in one of my mother's oil painting instruction manuals from the early sixties. Then I picked up a coffee cup with an image of Motif No. 1 and swiveled it around to read: "Once just an old fishing shack in Rockport, this little red shed became a popular subject of local artists, hence the name Motif No. 1. Visitors the world over have made it the most photographed and painted building in the world." [Ceramic coffee cup, M-Ware, China, undated]

Maybe I was feeling defensive, but this is when the skepticism began to set in. The most photographed and painted building in the world? Really? Why should I believe a coffee cup? I mean, where were the references?

I obsessed about my total ignorance of Motif No. 1 for several days but, after doing some investigating, began feeling better about myself. First of all, Motif No. 1—while not exactly a has-been—is only a shade of its former self, its true glory days extending from the 1920s to the Second World War. Secondly, all the claims about it being the most painted structure in the world seemed to lack hard evidence. How could anyone even document a claim like that? Was there a twenty-four-hour sentry on duty in the harbormaster's office, making hash marks in a thick loose-leaf notebook and then comparing totals with those of a French counterpart within eyeshot of the Eiffel Tower? Was there a certificate locked in a vault in Rockport Town Hall from an "International Bureau for Registration and Documentation of Small Town Claims and Boasts"?

In truth, I probably wouldn't have purchased the coffee cup had it read simply: "Motif No. 1: A Lot of People Take Pictures and Paint It." The sort of hype on the coffee cup, though I didn't realize it at the time, is part of the larger mythology surrounding the Motif and has more than passing relevance to this story. In an effort to confirm the Motif's claim to fame as well as justify my ignorance, I sifted through numerous newspaper and magazine accounts about it, most of which were feature stories that typically adopted a breezy and facetious tone. An AP account from May 18, 1959, for example, asserted that artists "think it's the most valuable building in the nation not excepting Fort Knox or the United States mint."[1]

The purveyors of hard news would always be a bit more guarded, and we can seek no better source than the *New York Times*. For instance, in a June 21, 1951 feature, journalist Richard Faye Warner reported: "Motif Number One is an old fish house, stuck on the end of a granite jetty that sticks out into the harbor, and the claim is that it has been painted by more artists—good, bad, and indifferent—than any other 'motif' in this country."[2] Warner is clear to recognize "the claim" as such and, with even more caution, specifies that the comparison is with any other "motif" in this country. Another hedge from the *Times* can be found in an article by Meyer Berger from August 31, 1947. Mr. Berger circumspectly reported: "The old red shack at the end of Rockport's dock is said to be the most photographed and painted building of its size in America."[3] Again we find the initial disclaimer of "is said to be," restricted even further by the crucial qualifier "of its size." I can be quite specific here, adding the pertinent information that the gross area of Motif No. 1 is 752 square feet on the first floor and 256 square feet on the finished half-story, for a total of 1,008 square feet.

Neither Messrs. Berger nor Warner was hanging himself out on much of a journalistic limb, and I can relate to the vague sense of discomfiture they must have felt when trying to play it straight in matters Motif. Undeniably, Motif No. 1 was associated with serious art, but, as you will see, its history was also characterized by serious shenanigans, and it's sometimes difficult to determine which contributed more substantially to its notoriety.

Secondary evidence that the Motif's fame might be a bit overblown appeared twice in 1988, when the *Gloucester Daily Times* reported that images of Motif No. 1 had been spotted in advertisements for towns in Connecticut, Rhode Island, Virginia Beach, Cape Cod and Maine.[4] Perhaps the most egregious example of Motif misappropriation was reported in November 1962, when a photograph of the Rockport fish shack was used in a chamber of commerce brochure for Portland, Maine.[5] *Boston Globe* coverage of the identity theft concluded with: "If anything will outrage the residents of Rockport, it will be for someone not to recognize Motif No. 1. Hmmpf."[6]

Does it not stand to reason that if the Motif could be used to advertise different places along the eastern seaboard, its association with Rockport is not universally known? Or that it's not recognized as anything other than a generic fish house on a pier somewhere along some coast? Should someone—hypothetically, let's say, from Kansas—be embarrassed by never having heard of Motif No. 1?

I was becoming confident that it did stand to reason. No offense to the town of Rockport, but geocentricity is not an uncommon characteristic of small and large towns alike. Moreover, while any tourists who have visited Rockport assuredly have encountered its most famous symbol, a lot of folks still haven't visited.

And then there is the matter of the postage stamp. On April 4, 2002, the United States Postal Service released its "Greetings from America" series, a pane of fifty different stamps, each depicting a state and images associated with it in the format reminiscent of "Greetings" postcards from the 1930s and '40s. Massachusetts's stamp includes Motif No. 1, representing eastern Massachusetts, and the ridges of Mount Greylock in the Berkshire Hills as a scene from the western reaches of the state.

IMAGE 1. The "Greetings from America" stamp for Massachusetts, issued in 2004 and designed by Lonnie Busch. *Courtesy of Guillermo W. Pimentel.*

I contacted the designer of the series of stamps, a noted illustrator named Lonnie Busch, another midwesterner like myself who originally hails from St. Louis, Missouri, and inquired how he had decided to select the shack for his stamp design. He graciously responded:

> *Regarding the red fishing shack in the Greetings from America stamp, I chose it after researching numerous reference photos on Massachusetts. The image continued showing up in my search, so I figured this must be an important icon. Plus, because the image was for a stamp design, it also had to fit the criteria of a stamp design, meaning, it must "read" well at stamp size. The red fishing shack fit the bill on that count as well, due to its simplicity and elegance.*

In a subsequent e-mail communication, he added: "And thank you for the thumbnail history of the red fishing shack, which from now on I will know as Motif No. 1!"[7]

There it was. I read the e-mail over and over again. Even the guy who drew the Massachusetts state stamp with Motif No. 1 hadn't heard of it. Hmmpf.

Enter Motif No. 1

In Which the Narrator Makes Further Observations and Lets Curiosity Get the Better of Him

Even though there were no regular tours of the Motif, I assumed that there would be a plastic holder screwed to one of the walls containing an informational pamphlet about the full-time town icon. Of course, on that October day of introduction I found neither holder nor pamphlets but, instead, three bronze plaques. One is a memorial for Leon "Windy" Wallace, "A Great Fisherman and A Better Man," who was lost at sea on October 13, 1988. The second reads:

> *MOTIF #1*
> *Purchased by the Town*
> *Dedicated to the Fishermen and Artists of Rockport*
> *May 14, 1950*

But reading the third plaque was the real shocker for me, as I felt like the last person on earth to know:

> *The Great Blizzard*
> *Of 1978 Destroyed The*
> *Original Motif #1*
> *Through Public Effort*
> *And Subscription*
> *This Building Was Erected*
> *In Its Place Nov 26, 1978*

As if things weren't confusing enough, the existing shack was nothing more than a replica, a shack double, an iconic doppelganger! I could go on.

Curiouser and curiouser! as Alice might have said had the rabbit hole plopped her onto this wharf. So I walked the short distance to Rockport Town Hall and asked for the tax assessor records. Famous or not, the shack was real property, I reasoned, and wasn't likely to slip past the taxman. From the field card so kindly provided by Assistant Assessor Diane Lashua—who might not have been so cooperative had she known then that I would be a continual nuisance for months—I verified that the current owner was indeed the Town of Rockport and also that the appraised building value was $54,600—a paltry price for an icon, in my opinion—and the appraised land value was $368,000 (a pier extending into the harbor is prime waterfront, as any realtor will tell you). Myriad other details of minimal consequence were available, including the square footage, which I have cited. However, four particulars were tersely listed in the "Notes" section that revealed the shack in a more bureaucratic light.

> *Rebuilt 78 Public Subscr.*
> *Motif*
> *Red*
> *No One There to Sign or Verify Info*

That about sums it up, officially. The tax assessor's eyes are not clouded by fame and glory. Despite all the hoopla, Motif No. 1 is a town-owned property on Map 37, section 67B, no more, no less. But now I wanted information about the *original* Motif No. 1, and it appeared that the shack prints of the tale were buried in the cold, dark depths of the sea (Rockport Harbor is not all that deep, especially at low tide, but the metaphor is irresistible).

Stories and knowledge about the artists who painted the Motif past and present—much of it firsthand—are in abundance, as long as you talk to anyone old enough. But despite nearly everyone having strong personal attachments and associations with the Motif, most Rockporters don't know many specifics about their town symbol. Even the mundane query of "Who originally built it and when?" was seemingly unanswerable; or, more accurately, there were an abundance of answers, none consistent and none appearing more credible than another. This did not appear to bother anyone in Rockport as much as it bothered me.

Of course, we don't expect people to treat shacks other than carelessly, much less to document their origins or mention them in journals or personal correspondence. Historical references to the shack, and even the wharf it sits on, are few and far between and parenthetical when they occur. Even with the best of intentions, oral histories can be vague, incomplete, contradictory and just plain wrong. Had town residents at the turn of the century possessed the foresight to know that the fish shack they took for granted—if not outright ignored—would someday be of historical importance, they might have paid more attention.

This is not to say that enticing tidbits of information were not circulating in print, on the Internet and in conversation. There was the apocryphal-sounding explanation of how the Motif got its name, the story of the Motif parade float garnering first-prize honors at the Chicago World's Fair in 1933

IMAGE 2. A Motif No. 1 collectible with some practical application. *Collection of the author.*

and the alleged secret paint formula containing crankcase oil, brewed by the artist Aldro Hibbard. These tales are common knowledge and documented both by John L. Cooley in his 1965 *Rockport Sketchbook*[8] and by professional photographer and sometime historian Leslie Bartlett.[9] But there are gaping holes in the historical record and no real answer to what I considered the crucial question: why *this* particular fish shack?

In the end, I didn't just buy the coffee cup. I also bought a T-shirt, a decoupage ceramic coaster, a shot glass, the Sebastian model and a Motif No. 1 whiskey decanter. Also books about Rockport, loads of them. Finally, to compensate for the embarrassment at my initial ignorance, I figured I

IMAGE 3. A watercolor of Motif No. 1 purchased for thirty-five dollars on eBay, perhaps by someone really famous who forgot to sign it. Offers accepted. *Collection of the author (photographic reproduction by Linda A. Marquette).*

needed a painting of the Motif for my very own. Not that I was in the market for anything significant or valuable by the likes of such artists as Aldro Hibbard, W. Lester Stevens or Anthony Thieme. Any example that struck my fancy would do. It was the principle of the thing.

So I went on eBay and promptly bought a watercolor for thirty-five dollars. It is unsigned, but I have narrowed down the artist to one of perhaps twenty thousand reasonably competent amateur painters who might have set up their easels on the wharf over a period of four decades, more or less. I would like to think it was crafted under the watchful eye of a Hibbard or a Stevens, who might have taken the brush out of the student's hands for a deft and critical stroke of his own, possibly prefacing the flick of the wrist with, "And maybe just a touch more red here."

But by this point, I possessed a clearer notion of the three obvious prerequisites for Motif No. 1's status, each with subfactors that will be dealt with later. First, Rockport is—and has been—a town for tourists. Secondly, Rockport is—and has been—a town for artists. And thirdly, the Motif is undeniably picturesque, both aesthetically and compositionally attractive to the artist and non-artist alike. A view of the shack is unavoidable from all but a few select vantage points around Rockport Harbor, and with its paint job, the shack pretty much sticks out like a sore red thumb amid the otherwise muted tones of the nearby fish houses, homes and town businesses. Surely the fish shack would have remained anonymous had these three conditions not been met, but none of these factors, singly or together, explained things. They were necessary but clearly not sufficient. One doesn't have to look far and wide among the small towns and cities of New England to find the quaint and the picturesque. So I repeat, why *this* particular fish shack?

Approaching the question as an outsider had advantages. Unlike the locals, who take their fish shack for granted and have their own personal histories entwined with it, I could approach the subject with few biases or preconceived notions and an unlimited capacity for naïve and dumb questions that a local wouldn't dream of asking. Thus, I set out to tease away the threads of fact from myth and extricate true tales from tall tales. Like an artist, I would consider Motif No. 1 from various angles, in different lights and from changing perspectives, all to answer the question of how a humble fish shack became transformed.

And all my work would be land-based. A perfect fit.

Chapter 2
The Old Wharf

The history of Motif No. 1 or, more specifically, the wharf upon which it sits—nowadays called Bradley Wharf—begins in the year 1837. Not to befuddle things at the onset, but the fish shack would not be known as Motif No. 1 until nearly a century later, and the wharf wasn't initially called Bradley Wharf. Prior to the 1880s, Bradley Wharf was possibly referred to as "western wharf," "old western wharf" or maybe just "the wharf." For purists who insist that a pier projects into the water while a wharf runs parallel to the shore, the Motif technically sits on a pier extending into Rockport Harbor from the termination of the actual wharf, which is the *real* Bradley Wharf. In fact, there are nineteenth-century references to the Motif's wharf as the Northern or North Pier, but this was probably not popular usage. More likely, it was referred to as the "old pier" or "old wharf."

Since linguistic nitpickiness does not serve well here, I will use the terms "wharf" and "pier" interchangeably, as most do, including those town founders who bestowed a wharf moniker on virtually every "pier" in their harbor. To avoid confusion, I will refer to the North Pier when necessary early in the story but will ultimately concede to the popular usage of Bradley Wharf as the home of Motif No. 1. But the reader should remain ever mindful that said wharf consists of both a wharf-like segment (conveniently identified for tourists today by a green street sign and typically lined by cars parallel parked along the water's edge) and a pier-like component, the former North Pier (and home of Motif No. 1).

A Wharf Is a Wharf Is a Pier

First formed in 1809 for the purpose of wharf building, the Sandy Bay Pier Company was newly authorized and empowered on March 5, 1832, to make Long Cove (i.e., Rockport Harbor) safe and convenient for seagoing vessels. It was also granted shore landholdings and rights.[10] At their annual meeting in Gloucester on April 17, 1837, the members of the Sandy Bay Pier Company voted "that the Directors are hereby authorized and empowered to commence building a wharf on the Northwest side of Long Cove and continue making erections as they may deem it necessary and expedient for the benefit of the Company." On April 16 of the following year, the company voted that the directors were authorized and empowered to finish the wharf, as well as to borrow money on behalf of the company to defray the expenses involved.[11] The wharf, as Ebenezer Pool noted in his journal, "was built with an ell so called."[12] This is the pier-like portion of Bradley Wharf we care most about here, which has an L configuration when viewed from above.

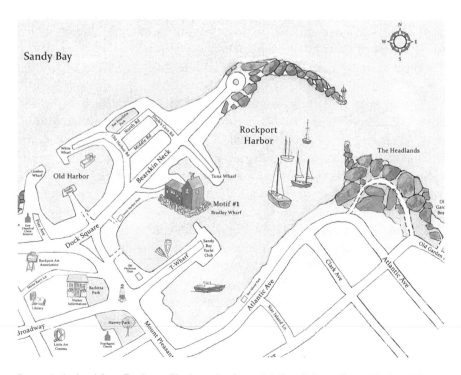

IMAGE 4. A visual for a Rockport Harbor wharf tutorial. Detail from *Town of Rockport Map*, by Mary Faino. *Courtesy of Mary Faino.*

The fact that what is currently called Rockport Harbor is actually the "New" as opposed to the "Old" Harbor doesn't make things any easier, so let's go to a map. Looking at downtown waterfront Rockport, you can see that three wharves—T-Wharf, Tuna Wharf and Bradley Wharf—define Rockport Harbor as we find it today. The relatively protected inlet of Sandy Bay to the northwest is the Old Harbor, originally known as the "Whirlpool," which contained a succession of the earliest wharves to be constructed in Sandy Bay, the first dating from the mid-1700s. Fortunately, we do not need to concern ourselves with the likes of White Wharf, Middle Wharf or Lumber Wharf, as they aren't part of this story. Even so, "wharf confusion" is commonplace in the present as well as in the historical record, so let's be grateful that this isn't Gloucester, which had eighty-nine wharves in 1880.[13]

Continuing with our Rockport Harbor wharf tutorial: the Sandy Bay Pier Company went on to build the Long Cove Wharf in 1840, which bisects the head of the harbor and was called Central Wharf before receiving the present designation of T-Wharf (after modifications gave it a T shape). Significantly later, in 1884, the company embarked on construction of its final New Wharf—which we will hear more about later—right next to the North Pier. New Wharf was later identified by its major fish proprietors, first as Hodgkin's Wharf and then as Story's Wharf, until officially christened Tuna Wharf in 1950, by which name it is still known.

Construction of both the North Pier and the Long Cove Wharf and the subsequent rapid expansion of fishing in Sandy Bay were only possible after the granite breakwater was built from the end of Bearskin Neck to partially enclose the harbor, a project that began in 1836 and was completed (sort of) by 1840 on the U.S. government's dime. Conveniently, the region's economy was booming in the 1830s, not only from fishing but also from granite quarrying, a business that began on Cape Ann in about 1824. While the ups and downs of these two major industries were not always synchronous, they were intimately related, as the artificial harbors at both Pigeon Cove and Sandy Bay (the two villages comprising Gloucester's Fifth Parish that would merge and split from Gloucester in 1840 to become Rockport) required granite for breakwater construction, as did the wharves. Before the breakwater, easterly gales drove fishing boats from their moorings and threw them onto shore, requiring the crafts to be drawn onto the beach for protection during the winters. The newly protected harbor allowed the fishing fleet to expand in both size and number of vessels and created a viable winter fishing industry, particularly for haddock, that previously did not exist to any significant extent. Importantly, the breakwater made wharf longevity possible, offering protection from the poundings of storm waters and high tides.[14]

Along with its slightly younger but larger cohort Long Cove Wharf, the North Pier was an integral part of the regional change in the fishing industry that occurred between 1835 and 1855, a period when Boston lost its preeminence as a fishing port while the Cape Ann and Cape Cod fleets expanded. In 1837, when North Pier construction began, Cape Ann's fishing fleet was less than half that of Cape Cod, but it would come to match it in size within twenty years. The populations of Gloucester and Rockport more than doubled between 1820 and 1855.[15]

The North Pier was a major player in these good fishing times. But the fisheries were only part of the rosy economic package. In addition to the granite quarrying, an entirely new industry had begun in 1822 with the opening of the first isinglass factory, which processed the air bladders from hake for use in the clarification of beer. The Rockport economy also diversified with the addition of a cotton mill in 1847, which primarily manufactured cotton duck for fishing craft sails.

Indeed, by the mid-nineteenth century, Rockport's future in every direction was looking bright. The *Boston Daily Evening Transcript* for Wednesday, September 3, 1851, described Rockport as "now one of the 'smartest' and more prosperous little towns in the State. It is fully up with the times—indeed a little ahead of them—and only wants a railroad, from the Gloucester station, and running to the extreme point of the Cape, to be handsomely fixed and furnished for this world." A decade later, the long-awaited additional five-mile stretch of rail to Rockport would be open for travel, financed by the town and public subscribers.

But as far as the North Pier was concerned in those heady days, it was really all about the fish.

Go Fish

The abundance of fish off the shores of Cape Ann in the first third of the nineteenth century seems the stuff of legend. Even prior to the breakwater construction, with limited vessel size and wharf facilities, the shoreline fisheries of Sandy Bay boasted an impressive catch. To get a sense of the place and the times in the late 1830s, we can turn to sea captain and historian Sylvanus Smith, who was born in Sandy Bay in 1829 and penned his memoirs in 1915 at the age of eighty-five.

Passing through the main street and coming into Dock Square, a busy scene is before us. At Long Cove there are many vessels, some fitting out for fishing trips, while others may be seen discharging their catch at the wharf, while several ox-carts are engaged in hauling fish to the flake yards on the uplands back into the village. Here, too, may be noted freighters, of which there were some 12 or 15, engaged in carrying the cured fish to Boston, New York, and other markets. From Pigeon Cove and South End, stone was being hauled in for the new breakwater which is being built, and the scene was indeed a busy one and presented quite a contrast to that of the harbor where at this time business is very dull.[16]

Considering the time frame of these remembrances—after 1836, since the breakwater was under construction, but prior to 1840 and the Long Cove Wharf—the "wharf" likely refers to what would come to be called Bradley Wharf and its recently completed projecting North Pier. The "harbor," in this case, refers to Gloucester, as it was commonly called prior to the incorporation of Rockport.

Rockport was not to fare so well during the second half of the nineteenth century, fishing and otherwise. Despite the fact that fishing was still the principal industry of the town, by the end of the Civil War the trend was inexorably downward. And by the time the cotton mill had been destroyed by fire in 1883, according to Captain Smith, "the fisheries [in Rockport] had dwindled to almost nothing of their former importance."

Turning back to our confined area around the North Pier and looking at the Bearskin Neck of about 1879 is not a pretty picture:

Here [Bearskin Neck] *are located numerous small fish houses, where hundreds of men were formerly employed in handling the catch of the many shore-boats that once sailed from here. Except for a few months in the year, Bear's Neck [sic] now appears like a deserted village. In the town are scores of veteran boat-fisherman who in earlier years found abundance of fish off this rocky shore. Most of the fishing is now carried on in large boats or vessels on more distant grounds.*[17]

Even though the fisheries in Rockport paled in comparison to their former glory, fishing nonetheless persisted to a significant extent. A pen-and-ink rendering of Bradley Wharf by marine historian and model shipbuilder Erik A.R. Ronnberg Jr. approximates the wharf's appearance at the time. Beside the old pier are two schooners (two masts) in the mackerel purse seine

IMAGE 5. *Bradley Wharf, Rockport Harbor, ca. 1880*, by Erik A.R. Ronnberg Jr., 1996. Pen-and-ink [4½ x 5½ in.]. *Courtesy of Erik A.R. Ronnberg Jr.*

fishery, along with their thirty-four-foot seine boats used to set the nets. The seine—a fishing net hanging vertically in the water by means of bottom weights and floats—had a series of rings at the bottom through which a rope passed, allowing the net to close around the catch like a drawstring purse. The mackerel were landed on the wharf in barrels, having already been packed and salted in the schooner. Thus, at least for the mackerel fishery, a large fish house occupying the end of Bradley Wharf would have served no useful purpose. Since aboard-vessel salting and packing of mackerel was not sufficient for long-distance transport, the barrels needed to be emptied and repacked with new salt and pickle, with weighing and culling of the fish into various legal grades. This might have occurred locally on the wharf (another advantage of a barren wharf with plenty of space) or after the catch had been shipped elsewhere on freighters or by rail.[18]

Take note of the open-sided but covered shed sitting on Bradley Wharf in Ronnberg's illustration, which would have provided sufficient shelter from the elements for barrels of salt or salt-brined fish, boxes of dry fish from the flake yards or other commodities in transit to or from the harbor. The actual shed on Bradley Wharf can be seen in a harbor image from a stereoscopic card taken sometime prior to 1882.

Rockport could not rival Gloucester in fish processing and packaging, but it was well positioned for the quick distribution of fresh fish to both Gloucester

IMAGE 6. A Proctor Brothers stereoscopic image of Cape Ann scenery circa 1882, revealing a shackless North Pier, background right (Central Wharf, background left). Note the large open shed on Bradley Wharf. *Courtesy of the Cape Ann Museum.*

and Boston after the railroad reached the town in November 1861. Shore fishermen from either city could offload their catch in Rockport Harbor and immediately head back to the northern fishing grounds, saving considerable time and money by not returning to their home ports. Nonetheless, five Rockport firms were engaged in curing and packing fish in 1879. About two-thirds of their business consisted of salt fish that were mostly sold to firms in Gloucester, with the remaining third of their business in fresh fish, principally cod and haddock.[19]

THE NEW WHARF

At a special meeting of the Sandy Bay Pier Company on June 11, 1884, Eben Blatchford advocated the construction of a new wharf on a ledge and ridge of boulders that extended from the South Road of Bearskin Neck, between the so-called "Little" and "Great" gutters, on the north side of Long Cove. At another special meeting about a month later, the proposal passed by vote, and specifications for the new stone wharf were presented at still another special meeting on August 6. A man named Charles Parker was the low bidder at $6,400 and contracted for the project, with a deadline for completion set for December 1884. Charlie evidently lowballed the deal, and in retrospect, the Sandy Bay Pier Company might have done better with the Pigeon Hill Granite Company, whose bid came in at a whopping $9,875.[20] We, of course, already know about this wharf from our Harbor wharf tutorial—the present-day Tuna Wharf. But the question is, why would such a project be considered, given the dismal state of the fisheries? What was Eben thinking?

The plan for the proposed New Wharf clearly demonstrates the North Pier as Motif-less in August 1884, as does an Essex County map from the same year. The first appearance of our shack on a county map would not come until 1899, along with multiple buildings on New Wharf. Yet another fish shack, which we will get to later, can be seen on the western end of T-Wharf in both maps.

The New Wharf was an expensive proposition that required well over the initially proposed budget of under $4,000 (a figure voted on at the second special meeting). It's telling that the vote to build the wharf only squeaked by with six in favor and five opposed. But the arguments in favor must have been persuasive enough to convince a combination of twenty-five or so fish dealers in Boston to sign up as investors. This we learn from Leander Haskins, who testified to the Board of County Commissioners in 1901.[21] Later, though, the Bean Town investors apparently came to their senses and sold their holdings back to the Sandy Bay Pier Company. But there was cause for economic optimism at the time, ample indicators for being bullish on Rockport. The citizenry was likely riding high for a couple of reasons, the first being the arrival of the steamship *Faraday* on May 22, 1884, which landed the first Transatlantic Commercial Cable (Bennett & MacKays') and established a direct line of communication between Dover Bay, England, and Rockport.[22]

The landing of the transatlantic cable indeed put Rockport on the map, but as heady as this experience must have been for civic pride, the increased

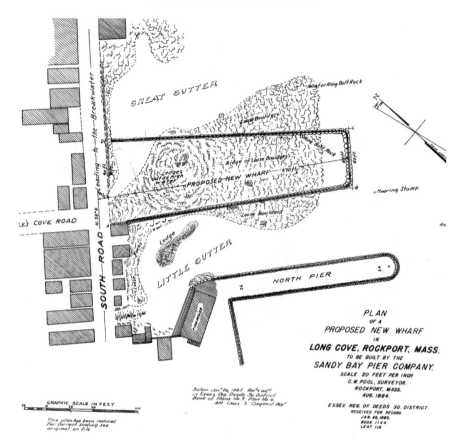

IMAGE 7. *Plan of a Proposed New Wharf in Long Cove, Rockport, Mass, to be built by the Sandy Bay Pier Company, Aug. 1884*, from the Essex County Registry of Deeds, Salem, MA.

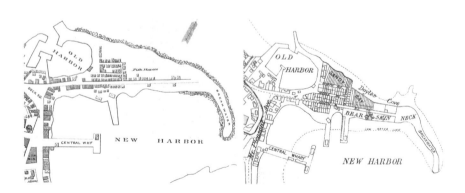

IMAGE 8. Rockport Harbor. Detail of Plate 20, *G.M. Hopkins Atlas of Gloucester and Rockport, 1884* [left] and detail of Plate 25, *George W. Stadley Atlas of Cape Ann, 1899* [right]. *Courtesy of the Cape Ann Museum.*

name recognition did absolutely nothing for fishing. But something even bigger was on the horizon. Enormous plans were afoot, plans destined to make Rockport Harbor one of the finest and nearly the largest harbors in the world. All that was required was a new breakwater—a really big one. With plenty of granite underfoot, and the government footing the bill…

Eben Blatchford must have considered it a no-brainer. Under those circumstances, how could the Sandy Bay Pier Company go wrong with a lousy 270-foot-long wharf?

THE GREAT BREAKWATER AND THE HARBOR OF REFUGE

Which brings us—or sidetracks us a bit—to the Great Breakwater and the Harbor of Refuge. A cautionary note: do not confuse the breakwater at the end of Bearskin Neck (then called the Long Cove Breakwater) with the Great Breakwater, sometimes called the Sandy Bay Breakwater. Wharf confusion is bad enough but understandable; breakwater confusion, on the other hand, is inexcusable. For this reason, I have included a visual aid that, had I been fortunate enough to peruse prior to my interview with a prominent Rockport sea captain, might have spared me abject humiliation.

One can appreciate the enormity of this project from the map by comparing the overall area of the harbor-that-could-have-been—which would have been surpassed in size only by that of Cherbourg, France—to the Rockport Harbor as we find it today, a relatively teensy-weensy inward coastal projection in the lower left corner, where both T-Wharf and the Bradley Wharf can barely be seen. Standing on the end of Bearskin Neck today, the non-myopic can make out the buoys that define either end of what should have been a visible 9,000-foot continuous breakwater with two branches enclosing 1,664 acres of water. The first buoy, a red one at Avery's Ledge, defined an 1,800-foot proposed southern harbor entrance with a water depth of at least 30 feet. The second green buoy, extending 2,700 feet to the east of Andrews Point, marked the proposed northern harbor entrance, with a depth of 80 feet. The future harbor at Rockport, Massachusetts, would have been able to accommodate 5,500 vessels.[23] Even the *New York Times* could imagine the bright future in store for the town, reporting on September 27, 1914, that "it will not need an unduly prophetic eye to foresee new steamship lines, or present ones with inadequate docking room, seizing upon this new harbor…and sending out thousand foot piers for their liners."

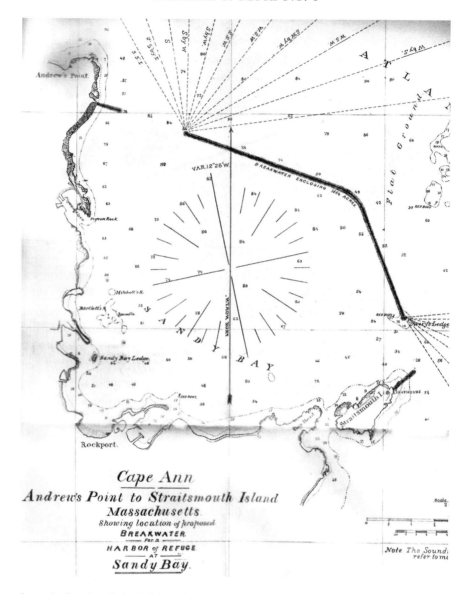

IMAGE 9. *Cape Ann: Andrew's Point to Straitsmouth Island, Massachusetts, showing location of proposed Breakwater for a Harbor of Refuge at Sandy Bay*. Map published in *Harbor of Refuge at Sandy Bay, Cape Ann, Mass.*, Harbor of Refuge Committee (Boston: Alfred Mudge & Sons, Printers, 1886). *Courtesy of the Sandy Bay Historical Society.*

The project, which had its start at a reportedly enthusiastic public meeting on March 29, 1882, saw fruition with congressional appropriation of the first of many contracts with local granite companies and the dumping of the initial load of stone from the sloop *Screamer*, captained by Albert Pittee, on November 12, 1885, at 12:26 p.m.[24] The boon (or, to more than a few skeptics, boondoggle) for the already rock-solid granite industry was underway. Cost was initially estimated at $4 million, with ten years of labor required for completion.

A whole lot of granite would be quarried, moved by horses or oxen to where it would be loaded on sloops, schooners or square-ended and flat-bottomed vessels called scows and dumped in the bay over the ensuing years. By March 19, 1886, ten thousand tons of granite had been dumped.[25] Meanwhile, back at the harbor, the New Wharf remained unfinished more than a year after the deadline for completion had passed, and discussions with the contractor were ongoing. On the bright side, there was likely a new fish shack on the end of the North Pier, perhaps even before that very first block of granite made its way to the silty bottom of Sandy Bay. The directors of the Sandy Bay Pier Company made no mention of this in their minutes, though. Evidently, they were distracted by more pressing financial concerns.

The first breakwater stone did not appear above water as scheduled on April 25, 1893, and after seven appropriations totaling $900,000 and thirteen years of construction, one-third of the breakwater was yet to be completed.[26] During this time, the directors of the Sandy Bay Pier Company were having some trouble collecting wharfage fees that were due on ice deliveries and were expressing concerns about the high tax rate being levied on pier company property. Clearly, their ships were not coming in.

And so it went. In 1904, roughly nineteen years after the first stone broke loose from the sling of the *Screamer*, $1,350,000 had been spent to transport and sink 1,800,000 tons of stone. With Congress abandoning appropriations, the last stones set down on the one-third-complete breakwater were dumped on August 23, 1915. And while just over nine hundred feet of the proposed nine-thousand-foot superstructure was visible, lurking beneath the mean low watermark was more than an additional five thousand feet of substructure, a jagged reef of rocks called riprap and more locally known as "Shark's Teeth."[27]

So the Great Breakwater was a disappointment of unfathomable proportions, and all Rockport had to show for its thirty-year granite relocation project was the most expensive man-made hazard to navigation ever created in the history of the world.

No matter. By that time, some artists in town had already begun to notice a particular fish shack.

Chapter 3
The New Shed

W hen Irma Whitney, Rockport resident and art critic for the *Boston Herald*, penned four arguably romanticized paragraphs about the shack in *Artists of the Rockport Art Association* in 1940, she was unwittingly chronicling the history of Motif No. 1 for the first time.[28] Her contribution— supplementary material included in the back pages of a directory listing meant to promote local artists—begins: "Seventy five years ago a fish house was built on Bradley's Wharf." Do the math and you arrive at 1865, the year that Lee surrendered to Grant at Appomattox Court House. Rockport, we have a problem.

Given the context, no one can fault Irma for tossing off an approximation of what was presumably a widely accepted assumption. In any case, with no specific birth date available, subsequent newspaper accounts would estimate the shack's age in roughly the same loose-handed manner, updating to account for the passage of years, perhaps taking Irma at her word or obtaining the guestimate verbally from someone else in town. Hence we find such references as "a seventy-five year old shack," a shack "now almost ninety years old" or a shack built "some years after 1840"—all reflecting Civil War–era origins and further blending oral tradition with the written word in a concoction of fact and myth that we generally connote as history.

A concurrent stream of oral history, babbling a few years before Whitney's account and equally inaccurate, established the Motif's birth year during the presidency of Ulysses S. Grant. In 1933, when a Motif No. 1 parade float traveled to Chicago World's Fair, the *Chicago Tribune* reported that the shack was about sixty years old, placing its origin to 1873 and crediting

John Buckley—the artist who was then renting the building as his studio and would shortly thereafter purchase it—as the source of the information.[29] At the Motif's dedication ceremonies in 1950, the *Gloucester Daily Times* referred to the "80-year-old lobster shack," near a midway point between the two prevailing beliefs and, as the saying goes, close enough for government work. The *New York Times* holds the record for being furthest off the mark, though, reporting in 1978 that the shack had stood on the pier for "a century and a half," a nice round number that dates the shack to 1828.[30]

Turning to the Library of Congress for a more authoritative opinion, we can find Motif No. 1 in the Historic American Buildings Survey (the "Monument" identified as "Bradley Wharf"), which was undertaken in 1938 by the National Parks Service under the U.S. Department of the Interior. An architectural rendering is indexed, the catalogue card bearing the information: "BUILT BEFORE 1880." This, at any rate, was the conclusion of Francis H. Brown, who is identified on the verso of the card and is not "close enough for government work" but is *actual* government work.

YOU SAY IT'S YOUR BIRTHDAY. WE'RE GONNA HAVE A HARD TIME.

We have already seen from a photograph from the early 1880s (Image 6), as well as from the plan for the proposed New Wharf of August 1884 (Image 7) and an Essex County map of the same year (Image 8), that our fish shack was not yet present on the end of North Pier. But the 1884 map does indicate a building on the western edge of T-Wharf that corresponds to a fish shack forerunner of Motif No. 1. A photograph from the files of the Sandy Bay Historical Society shows both shacks together at the end of their respective wharves and labels the T-Wharf shack as "Poole's Fish House." This demonstrates that the architectural design of our Motif was neither unique nor an original breakthrough, not that architects or architectural historians tend to bother much with fish house designs (otherwise, I would be citing a reference here).

While the identity of so-labeled Poole's fish house is not surprisingly opaque, it could represent the Rockport Fish Company, an entity that appeared in the Gloucester/Rockport Directories from 1892–93 through 1896 and the only fishery, fresh or otherwise, described as being located on T-Wharf (aka Central Wharf) at the time. By 1898–1900, the listing for the Rockport Fish Company is absent from the directory, and while the shack's

IMAGE 10. Circa 1890 photograph of "Poole's Fish House" (foreground) and the future Motif No. 1 (background left) on the ends of their respective wharves. *Courtesy of the Sandy Bay Historical Society.*

IMAGE 11. Circa 1896 photograph taken from the Atlantic Avenue side of Rockport Harbor. Note Poole's fish house (left), the future Motif No. 1 (middle) and buildings on New Wharf (right), as well as a large fish shack on Bradley Wharf at the base of Old Wharf (see 1899 Stadley map, Image 8). *Courtesy of the Sandy Bay Historical Society.*

presence is still indicated on the 1899 map, it was likely gone by then or soon after. Had it survived, one might speculate that Motif No. 1 could have had a challenger for fish house artistic predominance.

Clearly, the myth that Motif No. 1 was a Civil War structure has been debunked. But, alas, the first available county maps of any utility after 1884 are dated 1898–99. By then, not only had the shack been long ensconced on its wharf, but also, more buildings had appeared on T-Wharf and New Wharf. To narrow the gap of nearly a decade and a half, we must leave maps and photographs aside and turn to personal histories, deeds, tax records and even newspapers, if we really get desperate, with fingers crossed and do the best we can.

WALTER W. WONSON'S FISH HOUSE

Regarding owners or occupants of the Motif, Irma Whitney goes no earlier than about 1920, when the fish house allegedly "passed from the hands of George and John Tarr to Sweeney Hanson," a supposition that had been taken as gospel in subsequent writings about the fish house. For a reference earlier in time, we rely on information casually dropped by the *Chicago Tribune* reporter already mentioned: namely, that the shack was built by a Walter Wonson of Gloucester. And this is where the most heavily scented trail begins, as Walter Wonson's association with the shack is the only one that can be conclusively documented prior to 1923, although the actual extent of his association remains sketchy.

Walter W. Wonson was born in East Gloucester, the son of Frederick Giles Wonson and Deborah (Sawyer) Wonson, on August 13, 1858. Had he reached the age of, let's say, sixty-five, I would now be quoting his obituary for the most pertinent facts about the fish shack in which—at the very least—he operated a business in its earliest days. News accounts of "Wonson's fish house" would abound, including not only interviews with the shack patriarch but also photos of him posing on the wharf next to that shack of his, an old red fish house that was becoming a favorite motif for an emerging Rockport art colony. I would offer a cogent summary, quoting those articles extensively, perhaps throw in an old photograph from the *Gloucester Daily Times* and move along to the next chapter.

Unfortunately, Walter W. Wonson passed away at the age of forty-three years on Monday, April 22, 1901, likely stricken by a cerebral hemorrhage. He had no children—and thus no grandchildren with old papers in the attic to forage through—and was survived only by his wife, Sophronia Hopkins of Vinalhaven, Maine, whom he married in 1882, and one brother and one sister. His obituary, of course, makes absolutely no mention of his fish house.

Walter W. Wonson makes his first appearance in the Gloucester Directory of 1875 at the age of seventeen, boarding in the house of his father, Frederick, and listed as a clerk in his grandfather's fish business, the John F. Wonson & Company, located in East Gloucester. By 1880, he was in the fish business with his brother Charles F., operating on Rocky Neck Avenue. Apparently, the business did well, as on December 6, 1883, the Harbor and Land Commission approved a proposed extension of the "wharf of Walter W. and C.F. Wonson in the harbor of Gloucester, Mass."[31] The copartnership continued for about six years, since we learn from the 1886 Gloucester Directory that the Walter W. Wonson & Bro. Co. on Rocky Neck had become the Charles F. Wonson & Company, with the twenty-eight-year-old Walter now associated with the fish business Dennett & Wonson on Fort Wharf, Gloucester. The partnership with William Dennett, who was about ten years older than Walter, was relatively short-lived, since by 1890–91 they appear to have gone their separate ways while remaining in proximity; each boasted individual listings as fresh fish dealers on Fort Wharf.

The following year, in 1892, Walter W. Wonson made his first and only appearance in a Rockport Business Directory, listed under "Fisheries" and with the address of "Bradley's Wharf." This single listing composes the wealth of documentation linking Wonson to Motif No. 1, save the old standby—following the money to the taxman.

Image 12. Photograph of wharf and fish shack by Cape Ann photographer Martha Hale Harvey (1862–1949), circa 1890. *Courtesy of the Cape Ann Museum.*

The Rockport tax assessor records a new listing in his oversized roll book dated May 1, 1892: one W.W. Wonson, residing in Gloucester, the owner of record of a "Building on Wharf" appraised at $325. Notably, Wonson did not own the land under the building, which belonged to the Sandy Bay Pier Company. More notably, a structure corresponding to the shack did not appear on the previous years' tax rolls for the Sandy Bay Pier Company, making it unlikely that Wonson bought the shack from it. Corroborating this, I was unable to find any deed involving the sale of this property on Bradley's Wharf by the Sandy Bay Pier Company to any other party prior to this time. Which, I admit, doesn't mean there isn't one.

Whatever his involvement in Rockport, Wonson continued dealing in fresh fish from Fort Wharf in Gloucester until about 1898, when he became associated with the Gloucester Fresh Fish Company, "with whom he received an excellent position." Reportedly, he remained in the local office for a short time before being transferred to the office in Beverly and subsequently was appointed manager of the Boston office until leaving the company in 1899. He resumed his previous business on Fort Wharf, having also a branch store on Commercial Wharf in Boston, until his death in 1901.[32]

Taking the above at face value, we might be inclined to conclude that Motif No. 1 was built by Walter W. Wonson in 1891 or thereabouts—as John Buckley seemed to believe. But instead we must turn to the nearest equivalent of a Rosetta stone, if I can make the analogy, to help us decipher this inscrutable little history.

THE FISH SHED'S ROSETTA STONE

"Motif's History Recalled," appearing as a feature in the *Gloucester Daily Times* on May 26, 1984, was written by staff member Rick Doyle and based primarily on an interview with Esther Johnson (April 27, 1902–April 14, 1993), a former Rockport town clerk who knew town records and folklore as few other Rockporters did.[33]

The article commemorates a year that is "an important one for Rockport's most famous symbol, if one local woman is correct." The local woman being Esther Johnson, of course, the famous symbol obvious and the commemoration none other than the famous symbol's supposed centennial. This presumed the birth of the Motif as sometime in 1884, based on firsthand information received by Mrs. Johnson from a "very reliable person" who allegedly not only witnessed the construction of the shack but also worked in it as an employee of Walter Wonson. Our star witness was a man named George Poland, who died on April 15, 1955, at the age of eighty-eight.[34]

George Poland, who was born and lived his life in Rockport, would have been seventeen years old in 1884, so shack construction at that time would have been well within his realm of memory (though he might have been fuzzy by a year or two). In the 1894–95 directory, George L. Poland is listed as a foreman on Fort Wharf, the site of Wonson's Gloucester business, in addition to being listed as a manager of the Gloucester Fresh Fish Company in 1900, which gives him a definite connection to Wonson, who became associated with that entity in 1898. In 1901, Poland is listed in the directory as a fish buyer, in 1909 as a bookkeeper in Boston and by 1930 as treasurer of the Howard Hodgkin's Company on Bearskin Neck (New Wharf), a position from which he retired in about 1935. Without question, Poland had a strong association with Walter Wonson, and if not an employee of Wonson's fish-buying concern in Motif No. 1, he was at least someone with whom Wonson had more than casual dealings. So much for preliminary vetting.

Before I parse the account from the *Gloucester Daily Times*, let me express my belief that all newspaper accounts not recording specific contemporary events should be considered oral history written down. From that perspective, let us suppose for the sake of argument that Esther Johnson garnered her information from George Poland thirty years earlier, in 1954, the year before his death. Carrying the hypothetical further, in 1984, we would have an eighty-two-year-old woman remembering a conversation thirty years previously with an eighty-seven-year-old man recalling events from sixty-three years before that. And that's the reliable part. As such, the account is not without obvious inaccuracies. For example, Poland reportedly told Esther Johnson that the wharf under Motif No. 1 was built in 1817 and called Middle Wharf. I give George a pass on this one, since he was a fish buyer and not a historian, and I suspect this specious information may have come from Esther herself. Either way, it's a common instance of "wharf confusion" complicated by "harbor confusion," as Middle Wharf occupied the Old Harbor while the former North Pier, as we well know, is in the New Harbor. Nonetheless, this unpretentious news feature likely circles the truth closely enough to represent the most complete early historical account of our fish shack extant.

According to the account, Poland told Johnson that the fish shack was built in 1884 by a Boston-based fish dealer by the name of Seeger, who "headed a group of 20 investors who set up a fishing business on the wharf" and managed the business "in its formative years." Poland had to have been referring to a fishing business on the New Wharf, since this jibes with the testimony of Leander Haskins, who reported that about twenty-five Boston fish dealers had anteed up for the construction of New Wharf in the late summer of 1884. Seeger certainly could have been one of those dealers, though he remains coy when it comes to revealing himself in the historical record.

While larger, more substantive fish houses were eventually constructed on the New Wharf, given the construction delays involving the project initially, the investment group conceivably might have built a scaled-down structure on the adjacent projection of Bradley Wharf as a base for fish operations in the interim. Tantalizingly, a listing in the Rockport tax assessor's logs for May 1, 1886, records a "Building on Wharf," valued at $350, owned by the Boston and Sandy Bay Fish Company. Was this the same "Building on Wharf," appraised at $325, that appeared under Walter Wonson's name in 1892? If so, Boston and Sandy Bay Fish Company—a likely name for the original New Wharf investors—were the original builders and owners of the shack that would become Motif No. 1. This places its birth date sometime after August 1884 but certainly in the 1884–85 window.

The Johnson article next informs us: "After several fishing seasons, a man named Robert O'Brien became manager and ran the business until it closed in 1891." As feasible substantiation, a Gloucesterman named Robert O'Brien appears in the Rockport Directory as a Rockport resident and fish dealer during the appropriate time frame (1888–89), with his business location described simply as "Wharf." He owned no taxable property at that time, according to tax assessor's logs, and the year his business closed, 1891, approximates the appearance of Walter W. Wonson in Rockport as a fish dealer. Similarly, in 1892, Robert O'Brien appears back in Gloucester according to the directory, which lists him as a fisherman, not a fish dealer. He reportedly died at sea in the Gulf of Mexico on the schooner *Frances H.* in September 1909 at the age of fifty.

According to Esther Johnson's account, Walter Wonson, a Rockport resident, then bought the structure for fifty dollars and "operated a fish buying concern there for several years, [employing George Poland] until his death." Although Wonson was never a Rockport resident (he lived at 7 School Street in Gloucester from 1892 until his death), the account is a pretty good fit with documentable facts.

So the case is made—and a strong one—that the shack Wonson started paying taxes on in 1892 had been built about seven years earlier. Since the tax assessor valued the shack at $325 in 1891, Wonson indeed got a bargain if he only forked out $50.

In any event, from the tax books, the "Building on Wharf" became the "Fish House on the wharf," belonging to W.W. or Walter W. Wonson, until the records of May 1, 1901, the year of Wonson's death. From then until 1930, the fish house was the taxable property of the Sandy Bay Pier Company, first listed as "W.W. Wonson fish house" and then as "Building (Wonson)." Thus, the shack already had a name at the time of its rechristening in the mid-1920s, but one apparently known only by the tax assessor or his scribe, who continued to copy the name "Wonson" in the tax logs as an identifier year after year, even three decades after Walter W. Wonson's death.

We can speculate that Wonson leased the underlying wharf or paid "wharfage" of some kind during his lifetime. That the structure reverted back to Sandy Bay Pier Company ownership upon his death might have been the result of a contractual agreement, unless Wonson's widow sold the shack back to the company in an unrecorded transaction, as no deed of sale documenting its transfer can be found.

The fact that Wonson left no record of a thriving fish business in Rockport and never again appeared in the Rockport Business Directories likely accounts for others being associated with the shack during its early days. Still, from 1892 to 1901, Wonson was paying taxes on the little fish shack on the wharf, which likely he was either leasing to others or operating absently in conjunction with others. Since the Gloucester Fresh Fish Company makes its first appearance in the Rockport Directory in 1899–1901, its Rockport operation possibly utilized the shack. According to Esther Johnson's account, however, Wonson sold the building around the turn of the century to Henry Story, who also ran a small fishery where he salted, dried and repacked fresh fish.

A Story Fish Story

So we turn to the Story brothers, Henry and Albert. Descendant Story Parsons Jr. related that "legend says that the original Albert Story owned Motif No. 1 at one time."[35] While the Story brothers engaged in commerce at the wharves, there is no evidence in the tax rolls that either owned Motif No. 1, though that does not rule out the possibility that they operated a small fishery on the site as tenants of the Sandy Bay Pier Company. And while the alleged ownership by either of the brothers could be the result of "wharf confusion," their connections with the Old Wharf are worth exploring.

Albert Story (August 22, 1838–May 3, 1919) was commanding a fishing vessel by the age of twenty and presumably continued to pursue this livelihood until becoming a fish dealer. From 1886 through 1892, his fresh fish business on Bearskin Neck, in partnership with Warren Stevens, was listed in the Rockport Directories, overlapping with Walter Wonson's first and only directory entry in 1892. Another overlap is at Fort Wharf in Gloucester, where Story and Stevens listed business operations from 1892 through 1895, as did William Dennett and Walter Wonson, who were both operating at Fort Wharf (either together or separately) beginning in 1886.

Just after the turn of the century, Albert's brother Henry (November 17, 1840—November 10, 1907) was the proprietor of a variety store on Granite Street in Pigeon Cove, and Albert was his "agent" at the wholesale fish market on Bearskin Neck, H.L. Story & Co. At the time, Albert owned the barge *Margery*, while Henry owned both the schooner/freighter *Eddie A. Minot* and the sloop *City of Everett*. As local Rockport businessmen engaged in the fishing business, docking their vessels and unloading fish at the wharf, Albert and Henry could reasonably have been thought to own the old fishing shack. Even so, Albert Story's fish market was actually located on New Wharf—later Hodgkin's Wharf and now Tuna Wharf—in a building currently occupied by a fudge store.

THE BROTHERS (AND RENTERS) TARR

The other presumptive owners of the shack in the first two decades of the twentieth century were George and John Tarr, although again, there is no evidence from tax records that they ever actually owned the place. Rick Doyle interviewed John Buckley's widow, Marguerite, for his watershed article, and the former was under the impression (as was Irma Whitney) that George and John Tarr had been owners of the shack prior to Sweeney Hanson (with whom we will shortly become better acquainted and from whom the Buckleys used to buy fish). Esther Johnson confirmed that the Tarrs probably did operate one of the fish businesses on the site. As local fishermen, both George and John Tarr were intimately associated with the wharves and fish shacks in the harbor and could have leased all or part of the Motif in their fish business operation. We can fairly safely assume that Captain Tarr unloaded his catch at the wharf, perhaps selling it either himself or to Wonson and his cohorts or competitors in the early days.

George Henry Tarr (October 12, 1859–August 12, 1919) was a master mariner and owner of the *Lena May*, a fishing sloop built in 1890 in Waldoboro, Maine. Irma Whitney described the vessel as "the sharp nosed

Norwegian type with '*Lena May*' lettered in yellow across the bottle green of her stern" but incorrectly believed that Sweeney Hanson was her owner. In fact, after George Tarr's death, the *Lena May* became the property of the Howard Hodgkins Company, the large fish business on neighboring New Wharf. Thus, we have encountered our first instance of "wharf confusion" in conjunction with "sloop confusion."

Sadly, George Tarr, who was "one of the best known fishermen and highly respected for his sterling character," died on board his little fishing sloop soon after leaving the "Shoal grounds," nine miles off the Rockport coast. Local lore has it that the last time the *Lena May* came into Rockport Harbor, the master had suffered a heart attack and died, and the vessel sailed its way into the harbor by itself. In fact, brother John and crew member Alexander Jodfrey brought the sloop with its deceased skipper back to Rockport Harbor, docking at T-Wharf with its flag at half-mast.[36]

John R. Tarr (March 1869–January 22, 1924), who survived his brother by only five years, was employed at the Howard Hodgkins Company before his death, so he presumably had limited involvement with the shack on the wharf after the loss of his older brother.[37]

FISHY BUSINESS, INSIDE AND OUTSIDE

At this juncture we can pursue the overgrown trails of ownership through hard documentation, beginning with Sven Hanson, who owned the Motif and its wharf under somewhat complicated circumstances. But before doing so, we might consider what actually went on in that fishing shack during the last two decades of the nineteenth and first two decades of the twentieth centuries. While early photographs of the Motif's exterior aren't too difficult to find, glimpses of the inside are another story. But turning to Goode's *The Fisheries and Fishing Industries of the United States*, we can find a scene of fishermen overhauling their trawls in the interior of a Rockport fish house involved in the hake fishery, drawn by H.W. Elliott. Since the volume in which this plate appears was published in 1887, we can't rule out the possibility that the shack depicted here is actually the one we care most about.

Activities and contents in the shack and on the wharf itself would have varied with the season, depending on the catch being pursued and landed. The extent to which lobstering activities—such as gear storage, mending traps and lines and carving and painting floats and buoys—took place in

IMAGE 13. *The Hake Fishery. Overhauling the trawls in fish-house at Rockport, Mass.*, plate 53 from Section V (*History and Methods of the Fisheries*, 1887) of G. Brown Goode's *The fisheries and fishery industries of the United States* (Washington, D.C.: G.P.P., 1884–87). *Credit: NOAA National Marine Fisheries Service (NOAA's Historic Fisheries Collection).*

the shack is uncertain. For what it's worth, a brochure for the Charles F. Wonson & Co. from 1904 reveals that Walter's brother and earlier business partner sold codfish, pollock, hake, mackerel and herring but did not deal in lobsters.[38] However, a 1908 portrait of the shack by artist Harrison Cady (Plate 2) does reveal lobster buoys hanging out to dry on the side of the shack, providing evidence to the contrary. Given the shack's size, curing or packaging of fish would not have taken place inside, and in this regard, the shack on the old granite wharf was definitely playing second fiddle to the commerce on New Wharf during the first two decades of the century. The second story presumably served as an office for the fish broker or countinghouse. Jack Burbank, who would eventually lease this portion of the shack for a number of years, recalled in an interview that "Carl Johnson and his grandfather used to land fish on Bradley's Wharf and go up to the office in what now's Motif No. 1 and get paid off."[39]

One might wonder why Walter Wonson ventured to Rockport in the first place. Given the overall state of fisheries, the shack could have been acquired at a bargain (perhaps even the fifty bucks reported by Esther Johnson), and lease fees for wharf space would have been similarly competitive. More to the point, if full holds from Gloucester and Boston vessels could be discharged at Rockport instead of at home ports, a Rockport fish broker would have a competitive edge. Perhaps establishing a presence in Rockport was the means by which Wonson intended to get the jump on larger Gloucester merchants, shipping his acquisitions—after immediate care and preliminary processing—back to his principal site of operation at Fort Wharf on freighters or by rail. The shack itself, aside from serving as a transfer station office, could have served the usual storage and repair purposes or been leased, in part or in whole, to any number of fishermen.

Regardless of what was occurring inside the shack, income for the Sandy Bay Pier Company was generated at the wharves through dockage fees for vessels and wharfage fees on all goods loaded to or from the wharves. Dockage for vessels depended on size and ranged from five dollars per year or six cents per day for a four-ton vessel to sixty to sixty-five dollars per year or sixty cents per day for vessels between seventy-five and one hundred tons. Two cents would be charged for each quintal (hundred pounds) of fish, while wharfage on barrels was three cents for up to 200 pounds and four cents for 200 to 300 pounds. Boxes—considerably heavier at 300 to 450 pounds— would generate ten cents each. Charges were similarly enumerated for a variety of goods, including lumber, bricks, clapboard, coal, stone, salt and wood, while goods not specified were to be paid in the same proportion, the amount estimated by the wharfinger.[40] Subject to the approval of the directors, the wharfinger was in charge of the entire management of the wharves and docks and received payment from the masters or owners of the vessels, who were responsible for furnishing an accounting of all goods landed from or taken on their vessels.

During the early days of the Motif, James W. Bradley served as wharfinger for Rockport Harbor. Bradley had been in the fishing business with his brother William H. Jr. on Bearskin Neck until about 1892 and tendered his resignation as wharfinger on March 5, 1910, owing to "lameness and advanced years."[41] The brothers had been prominent vessel owners and outfitters of Rockport for many years prior, with their vessels "the largest that have ever been owned here engaged in that business."[42] The term "Bradley Wharf" was in usage by the late 1880s and likely came into the vernacular because of the dominance of the brothers' company or that of their father, William, who had been one of Rockport's principal fish mercantile businessmen a generation earlier.

Specific accountings from the wharfinger during the fish shack's first years, if they exist somewhere, would flesh out the considerable information gaps, but business had deteriorated significantly between the construction of New Wharf and the time of Bradley's resignation, and we can assume that the shack's leasings generated relatively inconsequential revenue for the Sandy Bay Pier Company. New Wharf, not surprisingly, received more attention at the meetings.

ATTEND THE TALE OF SWEENEY HANSON AND ROCKPORT COLD STORAGE

Irma Whitney informs us that Sven "Sweeney" Hanson was "the last Rockporter to use the property for fishing and to sail a fishing boat regularly out of the Old Harbor." Indeed, in the mostly forgotten past, isolated news accounts from the 1950s made reference to Motif No. 1 as "Sweeney Hanson's fish shed"[43] and "Sweeney's Fish House."[44] Visual confirmation appears in a 1923 book illustration of the wharf and shack by Rockport artist Lester Hornby entitled *At Sweeney Hanson's wharf*.[45] At least this is reasonably accurate, unlike press references to "Hodgkin's Fish House" (wharf confusion), "Monson's Fish House" and "Swanson's Fish House," the latter evidently a mixture of "Sweeney," "Hanson" and "Wonson." The extent to which Hanson's name was used locally in association with the wharf and shack is unclear, especially since Sweeney Hanson's fishing establishment, at least in later years, was located—no surprise here—on New Wharf. Of course, few today in Rockport have memory of that name, and fewer remember the man himself, an exception being a centenarian with whom I spoke, whose sole remembrance of Sweeney Hanson was that of "a stout man." This stout man deserves our consideration for a number of reasons, not the least of which is that he was an actual deeded owner of Motif No. 1. For almost an entire month, in fact.

Sweeney Hanson, born in Sweden on November 4, 1859, moved from Gloucester to Rockport in about 1911, when he is listed in the Rockport Directory as a master mariner doing business as a salt fish dealer with the Sandy Bay Fish Company in Bearskin Neck. In 1908, he owned the fishing vessel *Sylvester*, a forty-foot sloop boat built in 1899 in Rockland, Maine, and later he would be associated with the schooner *Gracie E. Freeman*, either as owner or captain. By November 1917, Hanson had achieved enough prominence in the community to be voted president of the Board of Directors of the Sandy Bay Pier Company at a special meeting, part of a management shake-up in which all five previous directors tendered letters of resignation.

The change may have been more tactical than adversarial, as minutes from a second special meeting held two weeks later reveal that negotiations for the use of T-Wharf had been underway "for some time" between George Perkins of New York and Edward P. Dixon, also of New York, who just happened to be the freshly appointed treasurer of the board of directors of the Sandy Bay Pier Company. A fifteen-year lease of T-Wharf at an annual rental of $1,000, and with a renewal option for another fifteen years, quickly transpired, setting the stage for the construction of the Interstate Fish Corporation's freezer/cold storage facility. This white monster of a timber building, Rockport Cold Storage, appeared on the end of T-Wharf in 1918. Although Sweeney Hanson was listed in the 1915 Rockport Directory as a "manager" on Bearskin Neck, and his directory listing was associated with the Story Fish Company through 1920, he apparently also had a managerial position with the Interstate Fish Company and, according to his obituary, was associated with George Perkins in the building of Rockport Cold Storage.[46]

The cold storage plant provided much-needed hope in a town where being down in the mouth was becoming an annoying habit. American doughboys were losing their lives in the trenches across the ocean. Quarry companies were failing and being reorganized. The isinglass factories were only operating a few weeks a year during the winter. And, most tragically, the Herculean project of the Great Breakwater was, both literally and figuratively, dead in the water.

Before contracting a Gloucester construction specialist named Paulson for the $120,000 project, Perkins had reportedly sent agents to scout both the Atlantic and Pacific Coasts and settled on Rockport—"where best fishing had the least chance for conserving its product"—as the ideal location for his freezing plant. Since fish freezing plants preferred fish only a few hours out of the water, such as those taken from traps along the shore rather than those brought in by the long-run schooners, Rockport fit the bill.[47]

Optimism regarding the project was short-lived, as the entire wooden framed structure succumbed to a devastating fire on August 2, 1923—the day President Warren G. Harding died—in the most spectacular blaze seen in Rockport since the burning of the cotton mill forty years earlier. The loss was estimated at $100,000, although "some" insurance was carried. The extent of the loss incurred by the Interstate Fish Corporation depended on the precise meaning of "some," but the business, hit by the slump following World War I, was hardly thriving, and at the time of the fire, the storage plant had been shut down for months and only handled fresh fish.[48]

On the bright side, we know that three years before the fire, on July 21, 1920, Sandy Bay Pier Company director John McGrath had called another special meeting to announce that Sweeney Hanson, president of the company, would no longer be employed as manager of the Interstate Fish Corporation. At the time, Hanson was requesting that the pier company lease him the buildings on New Wharf formerly owned by the Story Company, Albert Story having died in May of the previous year. Ironically, Sweeney didn't know that the Interstate Fish Company was the owner of the building. Still, he was apparently smart, or lucky enough, to avoid financial catastrophe when fire met ice. Rockport Cold Storage had gone up in flames, but Sweeney Hanson remained a well-established and presumably successful proprietor of the former Albert W. Story Fish Company on New Wharf.

The year of the fire saw much activity surrounding the wharf and its fish shack, specifically, three real estate transfers. But before untangling these, we might return to February 4, 1921, and the only direct reference to Motif No. 1 that I could find in the minutes of the Sandy Bay Pier Company. At the meeting of the annual election of officers on that day, in which Sweeney Hanson was reelected president, we find the following entry:

> *Mr. Hanson reported that he knew of a party who would like to hire the building on the old pier* [note the term "Bradley Wharf" is not used here] *and that he believes he would pay one hundred dollars a year for it. The wharfinger* [J. Loring Woodfall, who had again been elected clerk and wharfinger that day] *said we have a good tenant and he believed he should have the right to continue provided he would meet the other fellow's offer. On motion of Mr. McGrath it was voted to leave the matter with the wharfinger.*

Without names, we have no inkling who the interested parties were. But we can conclude that Sweeney Hanson was not occupying the building on the old pier at that time, and perhaps he never had. Possibly the tenant was a fisherman or boatyard owner David Waddell, who, according to family legend, stored oak inside the shack for his shipbuilding business.

FOLLOWING THE REAL ESTATE

Perhaps prompted by the business chaos accompanying the Rockport Cold Storage fire, the board of directors of the Sandy Bay Pier Company met on August 29, 1923, and adopted a resolution to sell its property to the Interstate Fish Corporation for $17,000. Separate, nearly identical deeds of sale recorded in the Essex South District dated August 29, September 24 and finally October 24, 1923, attest to procedural stutter-steps delaying the transaction.

But there was no time to breathe a sigh of relief upon successful completion of this land sale, since a subsequent deed of the same date, October 24, 1923, transferred the freshly acquired Sandy Bay Pier Company property, as well as all the property owned by the Interstate Fish Corporation (excluding traps, nets, trap boats, trap equipment and the *Gracie Freeman*)—but, of course, including a certain fish shack—from the Interstate Fish Corporation to none other than Sweeney Hanson. This arrangement had been cemented at a New York City meeting of the Interstate Fish Corporation stockholders on September 14, 1923, when Hanson had offered to purchase the property of the corporation, representing $17,000 for land and $16,000 for buildings, with the exclusions mentioned above. Finally, at the end of a long day, Sweeney Hanson had also procured the requisite $20,000 mortgage from the Granite Savings Bank to pull off the deal.

Less than a month later, on November 20, 1923, Sweeney Hanson sold the entire package to the newly formed Rockport Pier Company, of which he was a principal. Sweeney Hanson had only temporarily acquired the title to all described "under an agreement to hold the same for the benefit of said Rockport Pier Company until the same were fully organized."[49] And thus, the tale of how Sweeney Hanson owned Motif No. 1 for a month.

By 1925, the Rockport Pier Company's holdings included four fish house lots (valued at $200), Bradley Wharf (valued at $2,000), "Building on Bradley Wharf" (our Motif, valued by now at only $75), New Wharf (valued at $3,000) and "Buildings on the New Wharf," including the fish houses of Hanson and Hodgkins (valued at $2,700). Dockage for "owners of boats using wharves" included Sweeney Hanson, for the schooner *Gracie E. Freeman*, and the Howard Hodgkins Company, for the sloop *Lena May*.[50] By 1926, the only fresh fish dealers listed in the Rockport Business Directory were Howard Hodgkins, Sweeney Hanson and his son Sylvester M. Hanson. Sweeney Hanson died on May 22, 1927, and Howard Hodgkins on September 12, 1937, and the heart of commercial fishing in Rockport died with them.

The slimmed-down Rockport Pier Company hung on to the diminishing income from wharf activities and dockage and sold off its property in a piecemeal fashion over the twelve years following its organization. The last parcel to go was T-Wharf, which was sold to the Town of Rockport in 1935. Before that, though, on November 14, 1930, the Rockport Pier Company sold David Waddell the land in front of his shop, along with the granite wharf and, of course, the shed on the end of it. The purchase price was $5,000, with the Rockport Pier Company holding the note at 6 percent interest payable annually.

According to his grandson, Waddell first worked on boats at the Bishop shop in Gloucester before going into business for himself in Rockport, a relocation prompted by building material being pilfered at night and on weekends.[51] The "Waddell Carpenter Shop" made its first appearance in the tax assessor's logs under property listings for the Sandy Bay Pier Company for May 1891, with the "bulkhead" portion of Bradley Wharf employed for boat construction and launchings by Waddell (and later his two sons) for many years. This stretch of Bradley Wharf had been a site of vessel repair beginning at least by the late 1880s.[52] Waddell certainly had reason to purchase the property in front of his shop, since he had been paying wharfage on the same up to that point. And if he had not already been paying for storage space in the shack for his oak, he was now free to do so at no additional expense.

But this was the Depression, and times were tough. Waddell began leasing the fish shack to artist John M. Buckley to operate an art studio about 1931, and on December 28, 1933, Waddell sold Buckley the shack and the entire wharf upon which it sat for $2,200. The Rockport Pier Company held Buckley's mortgage for five years at 6 percent interest per year and refinanced Waddell's remaining property for $2,800, under the same terms.

But by then, Buckley's fish shack was known as Motif No. 1 and was already quite famous.

Chapter 4

NOT JUST ANY FISH SHACK

FISH SHACK: THE EARLY YEARS

Fishing business aside, our fish house was no precocious child star for either tourism or art. As early as the 1840s, the north village of Pigeon Cove, about a two-mile stage ride away from Rockport Harbor, had established itself as a watering hole for literary types that included Richard H. Dana, William Cullen Bryant and Ralph Waldo Emerson. Tellingly, Pigeon Cove had its own tour guidebook in 1873,[53] while Rockport's two earliest guides did not appear until 1924.[54]

By the 1880s and '90s, thanks to a growing tourist industry that sentimentalized New England as mythically rural, pre-industrial and ethnically homogeneous (i.e., waspish), Pigeon Cove had become a full-fledged summer resort for the well heeled. The environs of Rockport Harbor, on the other hand, did not merit the designation of "summer resort," perhaps in part because of olfactory issues.

Robert Carter, who anchored in the harbor in the summer of 1864, made particular note of "the smell of rotten fish that filled the air," which

had been so disagreeable on the previous evening that we should have hoisted anchor and gone outside of the harbor to pass the night on the open sea, had not the fog been so thick that we could not see our vessel's length ahead of us. It was so unpleasant on deck, that, immediately after supper, we had lighted our cigars and closed the cabin doors, to smother with the fumes of tobacco the fishy odors from the shore.[55]

Something still smelled fishy at the turn of the century, illustrated by a story involving William Dean Howells. The celebrity writer and critic was evidently so captivated by the small boats in Rockport's inner harbor that he allegedly contracted to purchase (I suspect "lease") an old harbor-front house. Unfortunately, as the story goes, he

forgot to consult Mrs. Howells, and, with utterly inexplicable lack of foresight, he chose a day to bring her down for a view of her prospective Summer home when the fog hid the landscape and the rocks of many colors, and at an hour when the "friendly little boats" were imbedded in the soft, none too pleasant smelling mud of a harbor whose tide had gone out.[56]

Mrs. Howells vetoed the real estate transaction, and Rockport's opportunity to counter the partisan Pigeon Cove name droppers ("You know, when Ralph Waldo was climbing these rocks over there...") was reduced to "William Dean Howells *almost* slept here."

Sometime before 1908, the artist Harrison Cady came to Rockport for the first time on a motor trip and, unlike Robert Carter and Mrs. Howells, was sold on the place at first sight, perhaps because of that artistic eye, the atmospheric conditions of that day or a land versus sea approach:

When I reached the village and wandered about its shaded streets and winding lanes and viewed its comely white houses with their sun-splashed gardens, gay with many old-fashioned flowers, I was charmed. But when I chanced to find my way to the little harbor and looked out from Bear Skin Neck upon the sparkling waters of Sandy Bay, I felt as though I had suddenly stepped into the gorgeous canvas of a Turner, for here were ancient stone docks and picturesque fish houses, their shingles sides weatherstained and ragged from long years of buffeting by wintry gales.[57]

Yes, there was definitely artistic potential in this scruffy little fishing village—an irresistible picturesqueness lurking beneath the workaday surface. But the shack and its harbor would have to wait patiently for their due. Art activity on Cape Ann in the 1880s and 1890s was centered in Annisquam and Gloucester, the latter dominating the art scene well into the first third of the twentieth century. Art aficionados are likely familiar with the names and work of artistic luminaries such as Fitz Henry Lane, Winslow Homer, William Morris Hunt, Frank Duveneck, Maurice Prendergast, Childe Hassam, Willard Metcalf, John Sloan, Edward Hopper, Stuart Davies and Milton Avery—all of whom have Gloucester in common. Another thing they have in common is that none of them ever painted the esteemed subject of this book, and they seemed to do all right anyway.

So we've established that in 1884–85, artists weren't exactly gathered on the beach at the southern end of Rockport Harbor, easels set up and palettes at the ready, waiting only for the pigment on the newly built fish shack to dry before dipping their own brushes in some Venetian red. Even Gilbert Tucker Margeson, the first artist to set up shop in Rockport in 1873—who couldn't help but see the shack through the rear window in his house—didn't pay it much mind. He, along with another early Rockport painter named Parker Perkins, tended to look seaward for their subjects.

Perhaps it's fitting that the earliest dated picture of the shack that I've encountered, from 1908, is by the hand of Cady, a self-described "interpreter of its simple architecture and rich 'atmosphere,'" for whom the old red fish house "posed often."[58] (Plate 2) Cady—nicknamed "the bug painter" by the local fishermen—would achieve his greatest fame as illustrator of the animal stories of Thornton Burgess, which included Reddy Fox, Jimmy Skunk and, most notably, Peter Rabbit. Though remaining very much a New Yorker during the winter, Cady was a stalwart of the Rockport art colony and imprinted his unique sensibility and illustrative style on representations of the shack that he loved. (Plates 3 and 4) And, as if to make up for a past transgression, Cady purchased the old tavern/boardinghouse on Atlantic Avenue that had so tempted William Dean Howells.

Not surprisingly, Rockport's first native-born painter, W. Lester Stevens, would also find the fish house a worthy subject. In 1913, the year he graduated from the School of the Museum of Fine Arts, Stevens painted a winter scene of the shack and subsequently left a legacy of harbor views that often featured the landmark fish house of his youth. (Plates 5 and 6)

Other artists painting in Rockport whose careers began before but extended past the 1920s include Eric Hudson (in Rockport as early as the 1890s, returning after 1911), Charles Kaelin (one of Duveneck's Cincinnati painters, who lived in a fisherman's shack during the first decade of the century and remained in town for about twenty-five years), Norwegian-born prolific Jonas Lie (who lived and painted in Rockport sometime prior to World War I and then returned in the early '30s) and Harry Aiken Vincent (a native-born Chicagoan who settled in Rockport in 1918 and, unfortunately, is no relation to the author). Except for the paintings by Vincent, which prominently feature the fish house, the shack is merely an incidental member of the harbor ensemble in these early representations. (Plates 7–11)

Despite the plethora of artists in the Gloucester area, no legitimate exhibition space for painters was available on Cape Ann until William Atwood and his wife, Emmeline, hired Boston architect Ralph Adams Cram to design a gallery space on Ledge Road in East Gloucester. The Gallery-on-the-Moors was completed in 1916, with "the first exhibition of the work of prominent American artists who have painted in Gloucester every summer" opening on September 2 of that year. Included in the exhibit were works by forty-three painters; of their seventy-three total paintings, eleven were sold.[59] From "Gloucester's First Summer Art Show Has a Brilliant Opening," a review by F.W. Coburn that appeared in the *Boston Sunday Herald* of September 10, 1916, we learn that New York artist Guy Wiggins made the first sale. A three-column reproduction of this "carefully considered presentation of old wharves," entitled "Morning Light, Rockport," accompanies the review.

Is it not prophetic that the first painting sold in the first Gloucester gallery depicted what would soon become Rockport's signature fish house and wharf?

FLAPPER SHACK: THE ROARING TWENTIES

Thanks to the Eighteenth Amendment becoming effective on January 16, 1920, the Roaring Twenties may have been off to a bad start, but Rockport took Prohibition in stride with a major surge in the artist population. Sometime summer painters, annual summer painters and resident painters all flocked to Rockport in droves, bringing students and a steadily growing stream of art patrons and gawkers in their wake. The growth of Rockport as an art colony in the 1920s was both unprecedented and astounding.

Observers at the beginning of the boom recognized something big was happening. A news feature appearing six months into Prohibition noted, "This summer they [artists] are there in such numbers as to promise the establishment of a permanent art colony of importance."[60] W. Lester Stevens, writing about his hometown "Artists' Paradise" the following year, would recount that "there were about 45 painters and students here [in 1920], with a promise of about twice that number this year," also estimating that "no less than six hundred artists and students come to Cape Ann each year now."[61] The wharves at Rockport, he said, were "always a Mecca."

Significantly, the wharves had more going for them than artistic appeal; not only were they spacious enough to accommodate forty or fifty painters at a time, but they were also public property. Not all local scenes were as easily accessible. Consider a picturesque cluster of lobster shacks on the shoreline below Atlantic Avenue, called Star Island, which were also victims of the Blizzard of '78. Known as Motif No. 2 by painters in the '30s, the composition could only be painted to best advantage at low tide, and beach space was limited. So, for a number of reasons—including practical and logistical ones—our fish shack was the preferred initial motif to be painted when someone came to town.

Wharves and compelling subject matter aside, Rockport had all the necessary ingredients for the care and nurturing of artists, starting with availability of cheap space. With the decline of fishing, plenty of decaying buildings and small fish houses and lobster shacks were available for rent or purchase, not to mention old barns, livery stables and factories. The shanties on Bearskin Neck were rapidly repaired and fitted up for artists as camps and studios. As an emerging colony, Rockport also benefited from the convenient access created by the growth of car travel during the interwar period: by 1920, there were about eight million registered cars in the United States, and that number would rise to nearly twenty-three million over the decade.[62]

Although a critical mass of itinerant and permanent art talent was already present in town, it took one particular painter to assume the role of standard-bearer of the colony for years to come, that man being one Aldro (short for Aldrovandi) T. (for Thomas) Hibbard. Hibbard attended the Mass Normal School beginning in 1906, continued his training at the Boston Museum of Fine Arts School and, after his Paige Traveling Fellowship of 1913 was abbreviated by the war, returned stateside in 1914 to paint winters in Vermont and summers in Provincetown. Apparently convinced by Rockport artist Charles R. Knapp to forgo Provincetown for Rockport, Hibbard arrived in the summer of 1920 and promptly rented space to establish a summer art school.[63]

Hibbard would become the heart and soul of Rockport as both a leading citizen and a leading artist. (Plates 12 and 13) Not only was he the president of the Rockport Art Association from 1927 through 1942, a parks commissioner, a representative of the Rockport Board of Trade and founder, player and manager of the Rockport baseball team—with which he was associated for thirty-six years—Aldro Hibbard also became one of the most famous landscape artists in the country, known especially for his winter scenes. His first class of students that summer included a number of World

War veterans whose art studies were aided by government subsidies. Among them was John Michael Buckley, six years his junior and with particular relevance to our story.

AN ART COLONY IS OFFICIALLY BORN

On July 22, 1921, fifty or so artists met in Aldro Hibbard's studio and formed the Rockport Art Association, which was confined to Rockport residents or "those centering in Rockport for the season."[64] Officers included Harry Vincent as president, Hibbard as treasurer and W. Lester Stevens as a member of the executive committee. In addition to agreeing to form the group, the organizers decided to hold an Art Week from August 17 to 27 in the vestry of the Congregational church. Musical and other entertainment events were also planned, as well as a costume ball.

The subsequent year would see the formation of two art associations in Gloucester: the North Shore Arts Association (with juried exhibitions) and the Gloucester Society of Artists (with non-juried shows and both modernists and more traditional artists participating). But by this time, the fledgling Rockport association was already making plans for a permanent building fund. Additionally, for the second annual Rockport exhibit, the association members were planning publicity in the Boston, Lynn and Salem papers, placing posters in establishments throughout Cape Ann and making sure the artist week was well advertised in Ipswich, Newburyport, Portsmouth and along the tourist routes to the north.[65]

The artistic boundaries between Gloucester and Rockport were porous. Hibbard, Hudson and Vincent regularly exhibited with the North Shore Arts Association, where Hibbard was on the board of trustees. Members of both colonies exhibited together in Boston—for example, at the Guild of Boston Artists shows or during Boston Art Week at the Gallery of Jordan Marsh—and permanent residents of Gloucester, such as the greatly admired Frederick J. Mulhaupt, would become closely associated with their Rockport colleagues. (Plate 14) But the Rockport group, led by the energetic Hibbard, was quickly developing an identity of its own, with a reputation for collegial artists working and socializing together that was both attractive to newcomers and good for selling art.

Other artists painting during this period include Yarnell Abbott, a Philadelphia lawyer who would serve as president of the Rockport Art Association in 1924 and 1925; Charles Gruppé, who set up shop on Bearskin

Neck with his son Emil in 1925 (Emil would move and establish himself in Rocky Neck in 1929); Carl Peters, from Rochester, who became a regular visitor in 1925 and moved to Rockport in 1927; H. Boylston Dummer, who left the Provincetown colony in favor of Rockport; William McNulty and Gifford Beal from New York City; the German-born inveterate yachtsman Max Kuehne; Galen Perrett from New Jersey; and Otis Cook, who converted part of the Waddell boatyards property into a home, shop and exhibition space. (Plates 15–18)

By 1930, the Rockport Art Association had raised the funds to acquire and renovate the Old Tavern, a Revolutionary War–era tavern at 12 Main Street that would serve as the association's permanent home. Moreover, Rockport had emerged as Gloucester's legitimate rival. *Boston Globe* art critic A.J. Philpott opined that not only had Rockport become "one of the great Summer art centers of the Atlantic Coast" and "a magnet for literary and educational people, and naturally for art students," but also that the Rockport Art Association had become "one of the foremost and most important of the Summer art organizations…and a vital factor in the

IMAGE 14. Photograph of fishermen mending nets on Bradley Wharf while a female artist paints the wharf and fish house, taken between 1918 and 1923 based on the presence of the Rockport Cold Storage Company on the right edge of the picture. *Courtesy of the Sandy Bay Historical Society.*

Summer—and Winter—life of the town." He also considered those old wharves around the little harbor to be "the most picturesque wharves on the coast...the fishing boats, the dories, the fish houses and the fishermen completing the harbor picture."[66]

Speaking of wharves, since Philpott has again brought them up, let's review our wharf tutorial from chapter two. If one discounts the three empty wharfs in the Old Harbor—which couldn't accommodate large vessels and held relatively little artistic interest—one is left with four wharves in the harbor proper, or three, if you include the old North Pier as an extension of Bradley Wharf. The view of one of the remaining wharves (New Wharf) is partially blocked by the old pier when looking from the southwest, and the third wharf (T-Wharf) had an ungainly fish-freezing facility on it, at least until 1923. Which made one particular old wharf with one particular fish shack a hot commodity.

But giving credit where due, the fish shack possessed undisputable visual appeal, with the ensemble of wharf, shack and boats being especially picturesque. But don't take my word for it; take it from Anthony Thieme, the Dutch-born artist who moved to Rockport in 1929 and would ultimately paint the shack more times, and with greater commercial success, than anyone else:

> *There are so few of these dark old buildings remaining in this quaint seaport town that so typical a one as this standing lonely and dark against a light sea and sky is a target for many painters. The harmony and subtlety of coloring has a depth and character that appeal to many art lovers, as does the accuracy and ease of draughtsmanship. The boats lying at the wharf glide gracefully into their place in the composition, the reflection of sails and masts painted by the brush of a connoisseur.*[67]

As one might expect, the shack would be a frequent pictorial guest at the exhibits of the Rockport Art Association. Take, for example, the annual exhibit in August 1923, in which the *Gloucester Daily Times* let it be known that "a number of Harbor pictures" were exhibited, "perhaps reflecting an encouraging market for them."[68] While it can't be said with certainty that our favorite fish shack was included in all the pictures listed below, the titles are promising. Artist Lester Hornby, whose importance to the topic will soon become clear, exhibited, among others, the black-and-white drawings *In the Harbor at Rockport* and *In Rockport Harbor*, which sound linguistically, if not artistically, very similar. Other featured works included *In the Harbor, Rockport*;

Rockport Docks; *Fish House*; *Fish Wharf*; *The Wharf* (two of these); *Snug Harbor*; *Early Morning, Rockport Harbor*; *Low Tide* (three of these); *Mending a Net*; *Sunrise*; *Water Front*; *In Dock*; and *Boats in the Rain*.

The fourth annual exhibit of the Rockport Art Association in 1924 is even more germane to this discussion. According to the *Gloucester Daily Times*, Charles P. Gruppé's charming pictures *Wharf at Rockport* and *Fishing Shacks* were the pictures perhaps attracting the most attention. Special mention also went to Frederic L. King's "delightful picture of the old wharf," titled *Light and Shadows*. Other listed entries that likely represented our shack included *Old Fish Wharf* by Miles Evergood, *At the Wharf* by Elizabeth R. Withington and *The Old Fish House* by Charles R. Knapp. But take special note of one particular entry by L.G. Hornby entitled "MOTIVE NO. 1."[69]

It's official—the shack has a name!

HOW THE FISH SHACK GOT ITS NAME (WITH APOLOGIES TO KIPLING)

The artist Lester Hornby is given credit for naming Motif No. 1, and justifiably so, given the documented evidence cited above, namely, the first appearance of that appellation being associated with one of Lester's own efforts. This is not to say that the term hadn't come into usage among the artists and students prior to this, which it likely had.

Nonetheless, I do have some quibbles with the generally told tale of how the Motif got its name, which is related in Cooley's *Rockport Sketchbook* as follows:

> He [Lester Hornby] *had taught in Paris, where his student's assignments included drawing standard subjects, or* motifs. *At his Rockport School he used the same method, with the result that many pupils, walking out of their classroom, saw the ancient fish house and drew it. One day Hornby, confronted with a new likeness of his architectural neighbor, knew he couldn't face another.*
>
> *"No, no, no!" he exclaimed. "Not Motif No. 1 again!" It's been that ever since.*[70]

Of course, "motif" was not exactly cutting-edge terminology or even brought to America by Hornby. Reporting on the first Rockport Art Association exhibit in 1921, the *Gloucester Daily Times* tossed the m-word all over the place, noting: "The landscape and marine subject *motifs* [italics mine] dominate the show as one would expect from the Cape. Figures and portraits are only fragile attempts and secondary to the familiar *motifs* [italics mine] of Cape Ann," and, "The Rockport Art Association is composed of painters who have found material *motifs* [italics mine] in Rockport."[71]

While Hornby may have uttered the words "Not Motif No. 1 again!" I don't buy that the name was coined in such an impulsive manner. For starters, if anybody was guilty of beating a motif to death in the early years, it was Hornby himself, as suggested not only by his entry titles at the second Rockport Art Association exhibit but also by his three illustrations and the frontispiece—all of Motif No. 1—in *Gloucester by Land and Sea.*

Even if Hornby *did* say "Not Motif No. 1 again!" I maintain that he did so in a jesting, even affectionate manner. After all, this motif was artistic bread and butter; and besides, why insult a student who is paying for drawing instruction? Nonetheless, I will grant you that artists at the time likely uttered "not again!" as a good-spirited inside joke. Look no further than the eighth annual exhibit of the Rockport Art Association in August 1928, when Herbert Barnett presented his entry *No. 1 Again.*[72] If an artist wanted to sell his work, would he denigrate it in the title?

But let's hear the account from Lester himself, who was a featured speaker at the Motif's dedication ceremony. According to the *Gloucester Daily Times* of May 15, 1950:

> *Artist Hornby, one of the outstanding artists in black and white medium in the nation, and a world traveler, said that years ago in his art classes he had referred to the lobster shack as Motif No. 1 in keeping with a European custom of naming the favorite art subject in that manner. He found that soon other artists were referring to the shack by the same name. He spoke of having painted subjects all over Europe, yet had "never found a subject so ready-made as Motif No. 1."*

Now, here was an opportunity—if there ever were one—for Hornby to retell a good story about a seemingly exasperated comment to a student, yet there is not the slightest hint of the version related by Cooley. But Cooley's story is a good one, in any case, and every legend deserves an apocryphal beginning.

YOU SAY MO-TEEF, I SAY MO-TIVE, LET'S CALL THE WHOLE BUNCH OF YOU OUTSIDERS

Linguistically, things are more complicated, and you might have noticed that Hornby named his relevant artwork *Motive No. 1*, as opposed to *Motif No. 1*. We're going to split some bristles here. While "motif" (accent second syllable) is defined as "a recurring thematic element in an artistic or literary work,"[73] a less common but nonetheless correct usage of the word "motive" (accent first syllable) is "a motif in art, literature, or music."[74] So, while technically "motif" and "motive" are synonyms, the former spelling, and hence pronunciation, predominates.

Despite the fact that "Mo-TEEF No. 1" is nearly universally accepted, the shack was originally referred to as "MO-tive No. 1" by the Rockport Colony artists, and to this very day, true locals and old-timers in Rockport refer to the fish shack as "the Motive." Some locals have bastardized the pronunciation, saying "MO-tiff" or "MO-tuff," acknowledging that the name as commonly written ends in an "f." I can't explain why this choice of synonymous terms was adopted but suggest that the "Mo-TEEF" version was too Frenchified for a group of artists who, although clearly influenced and indebted to European traditions, were determined to paint in their own distinctive American style.

If we can't exactly determine why the preferred word choice was "motive," we can do some linguistic sleuthing and determine when the change occurred, at least for public consumption by non-natives. About 1931, the *Rockport Daily News* (the Rockport section of the *Gloucester Daily Times*, usually on page two) became inconsistent in its own usage, employing both the "Motif No. 1" and "Motive No. 1" monikers within the same week in August.[75] In July 1933, the *Gloucester Times*, reporting on the Thirteenth Annual Rockport Art Association opening exhibit, described Antonio Cirino's *Fog in Rockport* as a lovely and gracious painting of Rockport's ever-popular *Motive No. 1*. In the second exhibit that summer, an entry by Anthony Thieme was titled *Wharf Motive No. 1*, which applied the terminology to the entire wharf scene rather than just the shack (and was likely named with an eye toward a non-local purchaser).[76] There may have been some ambiguity early on regarding whether "Motif No. 1" referred specifically to the fish house itself or to the overall "shack/wharf/boat" motif. In the Federal Writers' Project 1937 work *Massachusetts: A Guide to Its Places and People*, "Motif No. 1" is described as "the designation facetiously applied to the natural composition made by a little sail loft with a siding of vertical brown planks, which juts out into the harbor,

PLATE 1. My first photo of a humble fish house known as Motif No. 1.

PLATE 2. *The Old Red Fish House, Rockport,* by Harrison Cady (1877–1970), 1908. Watercolor on paper. *Private collection.*

PLATE 3. *Motif 1*, by Harrison Cady (1877–1970). Oil on board [25 x 30 in.]. *Collection of Ann and Gene Brezniak.*

PLATE 4. *Fisherman's Family Rockport*, by Harrison Cady (1877–1970). Oil on board [23 x 33 in.]. *Courtesy of McDougall Fine Arts.*

PLATE 5. *Motif #1 in Winter*, by William Lester Stevens (1888–1969), 1913. Oil on canvas [24 x 30 in.]. *Courtesy of Rockport National Bank (photographic reproduction by Robert M. Ring).*

PLATE 6. *Lowtide Motif #1*, by William Lester Stevens (1888–1969). Oil on canvas [24 x 30 in.]. *Collection of Mr. Kristian Davies.*

PLATE 7. *T-Wharf, Rockport, Mass.*, by Eric Hudson (1864–1932). Oil on board [16 x 20 in.]. *Collection of the Mosher Gallery (photographic reproduction by Richard Correale).*

PLATE 8. *Winter in Harbor*, by Charles Kaelin (1858–1929), 1916. Oil on canvas [28 $^1/_8$ x 32 $^1/_{16}$ in.]. *Cincinnati Art Museum, Source Unknown (Accession Number 1920.426).*

PLATE 9. *The Storm*, by Jonas Lie (1880–1940), circa 1925. Oil on canvas [30 x 45 in.]. *Courtesy of the Corcoran Gallery of Art, Washington D.C. Museum Purchase, William A. Clark Fund (Accession Number 26.800).*

PLATE 10. *Wharf at Rockport*, by Harry Aiken Vincent (1864–1931). Oil on board [11 x 15 in.]. *Collection of Robert N. Shapiro.*

PLATE 11. *Alongside Motif #1*, by Harry Aiken Vincent (1864–1931). Oil on canvas [30 x 40 in.]. *Collection of Mr. and Mrs. Thomas Davies.*

PLATE 12. *Rockport Harbor in Winter*, by Aldro T. Hibbard (1886–1972). Oil on canvas [24 x 32 in.]. *Collection of Dr. and Mrs. Joel E. Berenson.*

PLATE 13. *Grey Weather, Rockport Harbor, Massachusetts*, by Aldro T. Hibbard (1886–1972). Oil on canvas [24 x 30 $^1/_2$ in.]. *Private collection, New York.*

PLATE 14. *Low Tide, Rockport*, by Frederick J. Mulhaupt (1871–1938). Oil on panel [8 x 10 in.]. *Collection of Tom and Gloria Nicholas.*

Above: PLATE 15. *View of the Motif from Dock Square*, by Yarnall Abbott (1870–1938). Oil on canvas [12 x 14 in.]. *Museum Collection of the Rockport Art Association (photographic reproduction by Robert M. Ring).*

Left: PLATE 16. *Motif No. One, Rockport, Mass*, by Emil A. Gruppé (1896–1978). Oil on canvas on board [20 x 16 in.]. *Collection of Mr. and Mrs. Charles H. Brown.*

PLATE 17. *Rockport Harbor IV*, by Carl Peters (1897–1988). Oil on canvas [30 x 36 in.]. *Museum Collection of the Rockport Art Association (photographic reproduction by Robert M. Ring).*

PLATE 18. *Lobsterman, Rockport,* by Otis Pierce Cook Jr. (1900–1980). Oil on canvas [25 x 30 in.]. *Private collection, Paris, France.*

PLATE 19. *Motif #1 in Winter*, by John M. Buckley (1891–1958). Oil on canvas [18.5 x 22 in.]. *Collection of Dr. and Mrs. William Coggeshall.*

PLATE 20. *Motif #1 in Winter*, by John M. Buckley (1891–1958). Oil on board [10 x 12 in.]. *Museum Collection of the Rockport Art Association (photographic reproduction by Robert M. Ring).*

PLATE 21. *Rockport Harbor*, by Anthony Thieme (1888–1954), 1929. Oil on canvas [30 x 36 in.]. *Collection of Dr. and Mrs. Joel E. Berenson.*

PLATE 22. *Motif #1*, by Anthony Thieme (1888–1954), 1935. Oil on canvas [25 x 30 in.]. *Collection of Dr. and Mrs. Joel E. Berenson.*

PLATE 23. *Untitled (Art Class Painting Motif #1)*, by Joseph Margulies (1896–1984). Watercolor [17 x 21 in.]. *Collection of Mr. and Mrs. William H. Trayes.*

PLATE 24. *Inside Motif #1*, by Gunner Bjaraby (1895–1967). Oil on panel [12 x 16 in]. *Collection of Mr. and Mrs. Thomas Davies.*

PLATE 25. *Untitled (Motif #1)*, by Arnold W. Knauth (b. 1918). Oil on canvas [20 x 20 in.]. *Private collection (photographic reproduction by Linda A. Marquette).*

PLATE 26. *Motif 1, Rockport*, by Paul Strisik (1918–1998). Oil on canvas [20 x 30 in.]. *Collection of Robert N. Shapiro.*

PLATE 27. *Untitled (Motif #1)*, by Michael Stoffa (1923–2001), prior to 1977. Oil on linen [25 x 30 in.]. *Courtesy of Dorothy Ramsey Stoffa (photographic reproduction by Robert M. Ring).*

The big step forward is **FILTER-BLEND** and only Winston has it!

Yes, Winston was the first to recognize that further improvement had to come in the tobacco end, *ahead* of the filter! FILTER-BLEND is Winston's exclusive formula of rich, golden tobaccos *specially processed for filter smoking*. That's Winston's flavor secret—the smooth, satisfying taste that makes Winston America's best-selling filter cigarette. Try Winston!

Also available in crush-proof box

ITS WHAT'S UP FRONT THAT COUNTS !

Winston tastes good LIKE A CIGARETTE SHOULD!

PLATE 28. Winston advertisement, "The big step forward is Filter-Blend, and only Winston has it!" 1960 [13¼ x 10½ in.]. George Soini's red-and-white striped buoys make a nice visual connection to the red-and-white striped Winston packaging. *Collection of the author.*

PLATE 29. *Icon 1*, by William Bradley (1934–2010). Oil and 24K gold leaf on canvas and frame [11¼ x 13¾ in. unframed; 18¼ x 21 in. framed]. The Christian symbol of the fish, seen on the frame, serves here as an emblem of Rockport's fishing past. *Courtesy of Mitchell and J. Tyler Bradley, heirs to the William Bradley Estate.*

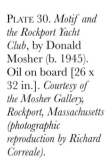

PLATE 30. *Motif and the Rockport Yacht Club*, by Donald Mosher (b. 1945). Oil on board [26 x 32 in.]. *Courtesy of the Mosher Gallery, Rockport, Massachusetts (photographic reproduction by Richard Correale).*

PLATE 31. *Morning Coffee, Rockport Harbor,* Tom Nicholas, NA, AWS (b. 1934). Oil on canvas [30 x 40 in.]. *Collection of Craig Knight and Teresa Lin.*

PLATE 32. *Motif Passageway,* by David Tutwiler (b. 1952), 2011. Oil on canvas [16 x 20 in.]. *Courtesy of David J. Tutwiler OPA.*

and a small vessel usually tied alongside, because the scene has so often been painted by Rockport artists."[77]

And here we must jump ahead of our story to the fall of 1933, the linguistic tipping point, when the American Legion parade float featuring the fish shack journeyed to Chicago. News accounts are striking in that the shack essentially left Massachusetts as "Motive No. 1"—noted as such in both the *Boston Globe* of September 23 and the *Boston American* of September 25—and returned as "Motif No. 1," according to the front page of the *Gloucester Daily Times* on October 9. And for substantiation, we only have to take a look at postcards depicting the wharf and its shack, which go from the designation "Stone wharves" or "Old stone Wharves" directly to "Motif No. 1" at about the time of the parade in 1933. The designation "Motive No. 1," to my knowledge, never appeared on a postcard.

A.J. Philpott, who began covering the Rockport Art Association exhibits in 1922,[78] persisted in using "Motive No. 1" in his reviews as late as 1938,[79] but from 1942 onward, the more familiar term appears to have been exclusively used in news accounts and reviews. Philpott himself apparently also gave in, adopting the usage "Motif No. 1" in a 1946 article.[80]

I liken "Motif No. 1" to a professional or stage name. More importantly, though, pronunciation distinguishes the born-and-bred Rockporter and denotes his or her personal claim to the special fish house. Anyone who refers to the "Motif" as opposed to the "Motive" or the "Motiff" (only pronounced, never spelled this way) self identifies as either "one of the newer people" or, of course, a tourist. The latter are welcome to visit and admire the shack, but it isn't theirs. They don't even know the right way to say it.

Chapter 5

Everybody Loves a Parade

O ur fish house is no aristocrat of icons. Befittingly, it did not introduce itself like the debutante Eiffel Tower, coming out at the Paris International Exposition of 1889. Instead, faithful to its humble origins and straight from the pages of a Horatio Alger Jr. novel, Motif No. 1 burst upon the scene as a parade float.

DOC GREENE'S BRAINCHILD

This seminal event in the history of Motif No. 1 says a lot about the way the Motif rose to the summit of all fish houses and also provides insight into the community of Rockport artists and non-artists that made it possible. If we are to believe anecdotal accounts, the story begins in a hotel room in Detroit, Michigan, in the fall of 1932, where Rockport physician Dr. Earl F. Green and Rockport insurance agent A. Carl Butman were attending the American Legion convention as delegates from Rockport's Edward Peterson Post No. 98. Having just witnessed the annual parade, Dr. Greene was struck with the notion of their lodge presenting a float of its own the following year, when the Legionnaire's Convention would be held in Chicago during the 1933 World's Fair. According to another account, published in the monthly publication of the E.L. Patch Company (manufacturer of Patch's Flavored Cod Liver Oil), Dr. Greene came up with the idea in conversation with Gloucester druggist Lee Comeau:

Everybody Loves a Parade

Their thoughts turned from pills and powders to the coming Chicago convention of the American Legion. Lee told the doctor about the Seine boat that the Gloucester Post had sent to the Detroit Convention. Surely, thought Dr. Greene, nothing could represent Rockport quite so well as the old fish house which has been painted by every artist who ever visited the town.[81]

That Dr. Greene had no prior knowledge of Gloucester's seine boat entry is extraordinarily unlikely, since not only was he from the neighboring Legion post but both he and Butman had been in Detroit for the 1932 Legion Convention.

There is also some question as to whether Dr. Greene or Aldro Hibbard actually came up with the specific idea of using Motif No. 1 as the theme of the float. John Cooley, in *Rockport Sketchbook*, reports that Greene came up with the idea, while his biography of Hibbard, written somewhat later, gives credit to Hibbard. Either way, Hibbard was consulted early in the process, especially since the lodge had to approve both the idea of the float and its subject. The proposition was brought before the Legion at a meeting on June 2, 1933, that included two representatives of the Board of Trade, members of the Gloucester Legion Post—including, incidentally, the druggist Lee Comeau—and Hibbard, who, not being a veteran, was not a Legion member. After the idea was favorably received, Dr. Greene became Float Committee chairman, and insurance man Butman was relegated as treasurer. Hibbard was assigned responsibility for designing and supervising the float, with John Buckley as his assistant.

While officially a Legion post project, the float was truly a community effort. Artists worked side by side with carpenters, artisans and a cross-section of volunteers of all stripes and backgrounds in an inspirational example of small-town America pulling together for a common goal. Money for materials was raised by soliciting advertisements from town merchants and businessmen for a publicity brochure, along with townspeople passing around a communal hat for individual contributions.

Hibbard's design transferred a harbor tableau of the fish shack and its granite wharf from the two dimensions of a canvas to a very three-dimensional old bus chassis. The old bus itself, purchased for fifty dollars, six flat tires included, had to be overhauled by local repairmen.[82] Buckley received painting help from W. Lester Stevens, Anthony Thieme, Maurice Compris, Hal Ross Perrigard and Richard Holberg. Included in this paint crew were two future National Academicians (Hibbard and Stevens), while the others were all highly credentialed and accomplished artists—not the least of whom was Thieme, who boasted an international reputation and a convenient background as a set designer. Buckley also had skills besides those of the bristle brush: prior to moving to Rockport, he had worked at the Museum of Fine Arts in Boston and performed a range of display-related jobs such as building frames and making backgrounds for exhibits.

Less illustrious but no less important contributors were also critical to the float's creation. Buckley contacted boat builder David Waddell, who gave permission for the chassis to be parked on his wharf and also gave the workmen use of his building, with its conveniently wide doorway. Waddell himself fabricated the masts, gaffs and booms of the boats moored at the reproduction wharf. Others were assigned the tasks of rigging the boats, making scaled-down lobster pots and figures of men working on deck and fitting the superstructure on the bus chassis, which required the expertise of local blacksmith Alfonso Thibeault. Even hovering seagulls were fashioned.[83]

The completed float, painted on homasote siding with a canvas skirting that camouflaged the underlying vehicle, was twenty-eight feet long and thirteen feet high and was fitted inside with bunks for four men. The shack was built to scale, although the rocky headlands at the rear bumper end were miniaturized. The chimney was designed on a hinge so it could be manipulated to allow the float to safely pass under bridges and overpasses. Headlights, however, were not included in the design, so travel was confined to daytime.

Official town sanction came in a special regulation, effective September 25, 1933, and found in the selectmen's records on the same date, detailing

IMAGE 15. The American Legion publicity float prior to its departure to Chicago. *Courtesy of the Sandy Bay Historical Society.*

the town's motorcycle officer as a special escort for the float's round trip to Chicago. Somerville mayor John J. Murphy, a summer Rockport resident, apparently was asked to use his influence with Chief of Police John Sullivan to get the escort assigned, and the chief consented after being told that the Rockport selectmen would approve it.[84]

The Rockport Board of Trade expanded and modified its existing promotional materials. A commemorative booklet for distribution along the parade route contained more than 120 advertisements, with virtually every merchant in town participating. A reproduction of an Anthony Thieme oil painting of the Motif graced the cover. Nevertheless, the fish shack was a representative of the town, not a headliner; the harbor scene was subservient to the town of Rockport. Spectators along the route to Chicago were introduced to a float of a "waterfront scene," a "fishing wharf scene" or a "Rockport Wharf," although the Legionnaires were more than happy to inform the crowds that the particular bit of Rockport on the wharf was known as "Motive No. 1" and why it was called thus. The commodity being sold, clearly and unequivocally, was the town of Rockport. While the parade float was unofficially christened "Simulated Motif," as recollected by Officer Jimmy Quinn forty years later, committee members of Post 98 at the time referred to it as the "American Legion Publicity Float," making its focus and purpose unambiguous.[85]

An Epoch-Making Trip. More Later.

After a christening celebration proudly sponsored by the Edward Peterson Post and a test drive through town on Saturday, September 23, 1933, the float and its entourage of cars left Rockport from Dock Square shortly after 7:00 a.m. on Monday, September 25, accompanied by the clanging of bells and tooting of car horns. The caravan included fifteen travelers, with John Buckley in charge. Other passengers on the float included drivers Simmy Mackey (the principal mechanic) and George Humalamaki (the principal driver) and "Professor" James G. Riley (the nickname due to his distributing pamphlets and answering questions about the town to curious onlookers). Two accompanying cars ferried nine others, including Edward Peterson Post commander Nestor T. Peterson, Dr. and Mrs. Greene and Buckley's wife, Marguerite. All travelers paid for the trip out of their own pockets.

The journey was expected to take five days, with scheduled stops in Springfield, Massachusetts, and Albany, Schenectady and Buffalo, New

York, to connect with summer residents of Rockport who would greet the floating scenery on their off-season home turf. The first stop for a celebratory reception was city hall in nearby Somerville, Massachusetts, where Mayor Murphy extended a welcome and a bon voyage, awarded bronze medals to the Legionnaires and received a large photograph of the float as a gift in return.[86] Hibbard attended this event but then returned home, leaving Buckley as the only town artist traveling with the float.

The road trip required substantial preparation, and the Float Committee went to great lengths to ensure a smooth journey. With the scheduled route along Route 20 and the plans for celebratory stops along the way, town motorcycle officer Jimmy Quinn had his hands full. Two Massachusetts state police officers were assigned to provide additional escort as far as the western border of the state, an arrangement worked out between Rockport police chief Sullivan and the captain of the Massachusetts State Police.

The first calamity occurred fewer than fifty miles from Somerville, in the form of a blowout that caused a three-hour delay and necessitated a new tire and tube for forty-seven dollars. By that time, the approaching darkness was threatening to spoil the plans of a welcoming committee headed by Springfield resident Mrs. Philip Bolger, daughter of the late George Tarr (who, as we know, was the original owner of the sloop *Lena May*, which happened to be one of the sloops depicted on the float). Mrs. Bolger and her party nonetheless managed a warm reception for both the caravan and the exhibit at the spot of the blowout after being brought there by Massachusetts State Police escort.[87]

Chief Sullivan also had arranged for support from the New York State troopers once the float crossed the Massachusetts border. This support consisted of a single officer riding along for a ways and then being replaced by another, until the procession had passed through the Empire State. From that point on, Officer Quinn was on his own, except for a short stint approaching Erie, Pennsylvania, when he stopped to telephone the highway patrol for assistance[88] and in the more sizeable cities, when local police facilitated passage. Quinn, who would subsequently be known by his nickname, "Smiling Jimmy," would lay claim as the policeman with the world's record for long-distance riding (about 2,300 miles). Quinn, deservedly, made the cover of a Harley Davidson publication in October 1933, posing with the town of Rockport's very own hog.[89]

EXPECTANTLY WAITING FOR WORD

Lacking instantaneous worldwide communication, the inhabitants of Cape Ann had to wait patiently for any news sent by wire or postcard, which would then be spread by word of mouth and reported in the *Gloucester Daily Times* the following day. Dr. Greene had promised to keep the folks back home posted, and A. Carl Butman anxiously waited in Rockport for word of any kind.

Consider the dilemma of the *Gloucester Daily Times*, struggling mightily to update the citizenry the day after the float's departure, with nothing more to relate than the disconcerting news, scrawled on a postcard and sent by Edward Reed, of a tire blowout. And thus the front-page story, headlined "Rockport Legion Float Runs Into Plenty of Fog," was followed by this remarkable example of journalistic bravado: "No official news has been received from the men aboard the Legion float en route to Chicago, but the float itself must have felt at home if the fog was as thick in the western part of the state as it was here, which of course it wasn't."[90]

Butman, the recipient of that brief missive and justifiably antsy, wasted no time in wiring Dr. Greene for news. Thus prodded, Dr. Greene sent Butman a wire the next day, September 27, reporting the party's arrival in Auburn, New York, in a pouring rain. One supposes it is always harder to be left behind than to leave, but A. Carl Butman was surely disappointed in Dr. Greene's commitment as a correspondent.

He likely felt even more slighted because, on the evening of September 26, Lewis R. Poole had sent a letter not to him but directly to the *Gloucester Daily Times* from Bridgewater, New York. The contents of the letter were published in the edition of Thursday, September 28, and included the following:

> *The float arrived here after epoch-making trip over the Berkshires, for our float zoomed over the hills, passed the detour at Chester, Mass., and climbed Jacob's Ladder* [a thirty-three-mile stretch of scenic highway through rugged terrain in the Berkshire region of Massachusetts, the first such highway specifically constructed for the new state-of-the-art automobiles in 1910] *like the gulls flying along with us. All are well. Gimmey* [sic] *Mackey and George Humalamaki are getting 35 and 40 miles an hour out of the motif number one. We are now at Bridgewater, N.Y. at the New Hibbard House, whose manager is J.J. Buckley—rather a remarkable coincidence as Aldro*

Hibbard designed the float and John Buckley was the assistant. All along the line people stare and wave. When we stop, everybody flocks around to ask questions. This is indeed an epoch-making trip. More later.[91]

If the coincidence of a Buckley-managed Hibbard House was to be taken for a good omen, engine trouble after the float's departure from Bridgewater would suggest otherwise. The trouble, caused by an "insecure valve rest," caused a delay of almost four hours and resulted in an unscheduled stop in Morrisville, New York. The closest spare part was in Syracuse, twenty miles away, so Dr. Greene had to drive there and back before the repairs could even begin. Simmy Mackey would later recall that the man who put in the steel valve seats promised to "eat them if they did not carry the vehicle 2000 miles." Once on the road again, the slogan for the crew became "Every mile is a smile for Dr. Greene."[92]

That Wednesday night, September 27, Poole wrote Butman a letter from Auburn, New York, at Dr. Greene's request. Published in the *Times* on September 29, 1933, the letter included:

If you could only see the receptions we get all along the line! Everybody is anxious to help if we need it. Today while parked in Morrisville waiting for Simmy and George to repair whatever the matter was, I guess about the whole town came to see us. Even the schools sent first one grade, then another, to hear about it. Professor James G. Reilly gave the talk and he was certainly right at home.

The editor of the paper at Morrisville is going to send a number of copies of today's edition to me at Rockport. All the boys are well and hearty and having a great time.

A handful of Rockport natives were fortunate enough to encounter the float unexpectedly, as these two snippets from the *Gloucester Daily Times* of September 29 illustrate:

A local party composed of Dr. and Mrs. Albert E. Tuck and Mr. and Mrs. Walter Tuck received a thrill when they passed the float in New York State while returning home from the World's Fair. The "motive," however, was traveling so fast that greetings could not be exchanged.

A pleasant, unexpected reunion was enjoyed, though, when Mrs. Chester Tupper of Springfield, daughter of Mrs. Laura Richardson of this town, passed the parade float in Madison, N.Y., and both parties stopped and visited for a quarter of an hour.

After the initial mechanical setbacks in western Massachusetts and New York State, things were indeed going well, with positive response continuing throughout the expedition. Saturday's paper, September 30, reported that Butman had since received no word other than a postcard sent by E. Morton Smith from Erie, Pennsylvania, where the crew had arrived Thursday night after a three-hundred-mile run from Auburn, New York. Communications over the weekend only included postcards sent to Butman and from Officer Quinn to his friend Percy Curtis, both mailed from Fayette, Ohio, where the party spent the night on Friday, September 29. Finally, on Monday, October 2, the *Times* triumphantly announced that the float had safely arrived in Chicago at 6:15 p.m. on Saturday, September 30.

To confirm his failings as a correspondent, at least perhaps in the eyes of A. Carl Butman, Dr. Greene sent the telegram with the breaking news not to Butman but to one Walter Tuck. This being the same Walter Tuck from above, who, heading east from the World's Fair on Route 20 in New York State, passed the float clipping along in the opposite direction toward Chicago. Assuming speeds of the two vehicles at fifty and forty miles per hour, respectively, we have the makings of a historically relevant algebra problem. But we can't linger, because the parade is about to start.

THE MARCH TO VICTORY

Parade day in Chicago was beautiful and cloudless, blessed not only by autumn's golden sunshine but also by a soft breeze from the south and west that swayed flags "like a multitudinous benediction."[93] At precisely 10:00 a.m. on October 3, 1933, Major General Frank Parker, commander of the Sixth Corps, issued the command to march. The procession included 350 bands, 200 drum corps and 250 floats and, trekking roughly a mile and a half from Michigan Avenue to Soldier's Field (where 70,000—some reported 100,000—spectators awaited), would take more than nine hours to complete.

The Legion parade was deemed the most successful in its fifteen-year history, with throngs of cheering onlookers lining Michigan Avenue in rows that were reportedly twelve persons deep in some places and countless more surveying the scene through windows of towers and skyscrapers. National commander Louis A. Johnson, who received salutes all day as he sat in the reviewing stand with other notables, declared a new parade record had been set, asserting: "There are 160,000 in it,"[94] presumably referring to those actually in the line of march. I am somewhat skeptical about the recordkeeping involved, since the *Boston Herald* claimed that the Massachusetts contingent consisted of 9,000 marchers, while the *Chicago Tribune*—while confirming that the Massachusetts delegation was the largest representation outside of the state of Illinois—put its numbers at 2,194. My suspicion is that the *Herald* rounded up slightly.

The Rockport delegation, sandwiched between the units from Marlboro and Beverly, took its place in line at roughly 11:30 a.m. and didn't actually start marching until about 2:00 p.m. Leading the delegation on foot was the uniformed Dr. Greene, followed by Officer Quinn astride the town's Harley, three color-bearers, two guards and two Post 98 banner carriers. Commander Nestor Peterson and James Reilly reportedly walked alongside the float itself and were assigned the task of protecting the faux wharf scene from souvenir hunters.[95]

The delegation had every reason to suspect an enthusiastic response, given the accolades it had received over the first one thousand miles of the

IMAGE 16. The American Legion publicity float during its triumphant appearance at the Legionnaire's Convention Parade in Chicago on October 3, 1933, with Edward Peterson Post commander Nestor T. Peterson waving to the throngs. *Courtesy of the Sandy Bay Historical Society.*

trip to the Windy City. Evidently, there had been some naysayers back home who had predicted that the float was not flashy enough to attract attention. But this was a minority view, and most shared the sentiments expressed by the *Boston Globe*, which opined, "It is doubtful if any float in that great parade will compare in picturesqueness or historic suggestion with the float from Rockport," and, going even further, forecasted that the float "will surely put Rockport on the map."[96]

An unbiased Chicagoan, reporting for the *Tribune*, gave the following real-time assessment from his observing perch in Soldier's Field: "Legionnaires from Rockport, Mass, are swinging by with a float that represents the edge of a fishing village on their stern and rockbound coast. It is as softly toned as a water color and is acclaimed by one and all as the scenic success of the pageant."[97]

Not to diminish the painstaking effort of Rockport's artistic talent, we might take a moment to acquaint ourselves with the main competition. The Legion post from Alexandria, Indiana, the self-proclaimed "Rock Wool City," attempted to substantiate its claim with "glittering floats representing winter scenes and built of the snow white insulating product for which Alexandria is famous." Reading, Pennsylvania, presented a float "full of coal queens," who were "very easy to look upon." Along those same lines, Berriou Springs, Michigan, entered an apparent crowd pleaser boasting its celebrated peaches, in this case represented by the kind of peaches "that can talk and that can blow kisses" from a float reminiscent of a "huge lacy valentine."[98] A Mississippi float bore a queen and her court, who tossed balls of cotton at the policemen guarding the curbs (I suspect in what might have been viewed a provocative manner).[99] Essentially, our model Motif found itself going head to head with cheesecake or, as the crew members would more diplomatically report upon returning home, "showy commercial affairs" that seemed "vulgar" next to the Motif.[100]

The following day, the *Chicago Tribune* published a list of the best of the Legion parade in an unadorned two-column article buried on page fifteen. The Commonwealth of Massachusetts had done itself proud. Eighteen-year-old Dorothy Slamin of Waltham, representing the Alexander Graham Bell Post No. 109 of Boston, had been deemed best drum major. And the winner in the "Historical float" category was "Rockport, Mass, with water front scene."[101] Until seeing this article in the morning paper for themselves, the float crew had been unaware that they had been awarded the judge's special recognition.

Miss Slamin, "the best twirling and high stepping drum major"—who thirteen years later would organize the Waltham American Legion Post

#156 Band and serve as its director for fifty years—upstaged Rockport in the front-page *Boston Herald* coverage. She was granted a single-column photo, the upper half nearly entirely filled by her high-topping drum major headpiece, while only two sentences were devoted to the float winner, described as "a reproduction of a familiar Massachusetts scene, a fish house and dock just outside [*sic*] Rockport."[102] The locals, as would be expected, responded much more enthusiastically: the *Gloucester Daily Times* devoted two columns of copy and a three-column photograph in the day's lead story.

Still, firsthand reporting was conspicuously lacking, since no real word had actually been received from the Rockport delegation, and the people at home were expectantly waiting for a long letter detailing the momentous events and experiences. Nevertheless, the story's broader implications were not lost on anyone: "The recipient of enthusiastic acclaim all along its journey to Chicago, the float will be pictured in hundreds of newspapers all over the country now, thus accomplishing in full measure its purpose of advertising Rockport," opined the *Gloucester Daily Times*.[103] Mission accomplished, beyond anyone's imaginings.

TRIUMPHANT RETURN OF THE ALL-CONQUERING FISH SHACK AND WHARF MOTIF

The float team had already made plans to head back to Rockport on Wednesday afternoon and was forced to decline participation in both a special parade through the fairgrounds that afternoon and a trophy presentation ceremony in Chicago's city hall scheduled for noon on Thursday. No arrangements for receiving any kind of award had been included in the itinerary, since the Legion post had been informed early on in the process that no prizes of any kind were planned in its category. Appropriately, though, Sylvester Hanson—a former legion officer and son of Motif-owner-in-brief Sweeney Hanson—was in Chicago for the festivities and was available to stay on to fill in at the last minute. A. Carl Butman's wife was also in Chicago, presumably part of a Rockport contingent traveling independently by train (and hopefully a better pen pal for her husband than Doc Greene), and asked to accompany Hanson to city hall as a representative of the float committee.[104]

Meanwhile, the float and its entourage began their uneventful trip homeward, during which they encountered no mechanical problems and made evening stops in South Bend, Indiana; Elyria, Ohio; Leroy, New York; Fonda, New York; and Marlboro, Massachusetts. From Marlboro, some of the party who could travel by night (that is, had car headlights) ventured home, leaving the float and a reduced contingent moored in Marlboro.

Since the exact time of the triumphant return to Rockport could not be precisely anticipated, the organization of the town reception was encumbered. However, Joseph Thibeault, chairman of the reception committee, did his best with limited notice, establishing an early warning system: fire alarms were to be sounded in town upon word that the float had passed through Salem. At about 11:50 a.m., the float sped down Main Street through Gloucester, boasting an escort of nearly a dozen cars, two state troopers and Jimmy Quinn on his Harley. By the time the float was approaching town on Great Hill, a greeting committee had assembled, including Thibeault, the Rockport pump of the fire department, the Pigeon Cove Combination Forest warden's firefighting truck and the hook and ladder truck of Rockport. The sounding of another alarm heralded notification of the float's imminent approach and a somewhat spur-of-the-moment celebratory parade.[105] The float and its automotive entourage made a victory lap via Granite Street to Pigeon Cove and back to Dock Square to meet the crowd gathered there.[106]

This huge crowd was no doubt a "happy and proud throng," but a later report that the gathering of celebrants numbered four thousand people—roughly five hundred more than the population of the entire town—may be the result of significant rounding up (as is becoming routine by now).[107]

According to the *Christian Science Monitor*, the exhibit that pulled up to Dock Square after the two-thousand-plus-mile voyage was "stormwrecked," with the fish house chimney "on the verge of utter demolition." Moreover, "the only sea gull that had weathered the gale, stood on its head clinging to the remains of the chimney by one foot."[108] Although the float was probably somewhat worse for wear, the *Monitor* has some credibility problems. In covering the parade earlier, it reported "A Post from Rockport, Mass. *rigged their automobile to look like a ship* [italics mine], suggesting the marine atmosphere of their home town."[109] And in its parade postmortem article describing the state of the chimney and seagulls, the *Monitor* article referred to a "Monson's wharf" on three occasions.

The Summing Up

A correspondent described the float envoys as flushed with their achievement "but nearly broke." The fact that financial concerns were never too far from the fore in these trying times was further implied by the incidental mention that, while Joseph Thibeault was making plans for a commemorative celebration, "lack of funds has so far prevented any definite arrangements from being made."[110]

The trophy made it home to Rockport the following evening, hand-carried by Sylvester Hanson, apparently without additional fanfare. Exhibited in the window of Joseph W. Thibeault's store on Main Street, it was described as "a very handsome piece of work, standing about 20 inches high, with three fluted columns surrounding a spread eagle on the black base, and a robed man holding a crest on which is marked the American Legion emblem in gold on the top."[111]

To substantiate that description, I was able to track down the real thing, a bit tarnished and rusty. Larry Story, a member of the executive committee of the Edward Peterson Post, found it for me among a bunch of sports trophies stashed on top of the television on the second floor of the lodge, lost in plain sight. The inscription reads:

Best Float in Parade
American National Convention
Chicago, 1933

Ten days after the triumphant return, the celebration took the form of a testimonial banquet at Rockport Town Hall in honor of the Edward Peterson float committee and all others involved in the float's creation and journey. An estimated two hundred persons were in attendance: Legionnaires, artists, members of the float crew, local officials and townspeople. Included in the evening's celebration—quite a jubilant and enjoyable affair, if the account in the Rockport section of the *Gloucester Daily Times* on October 19 is any indication— was the presentation of the trophy by Sylvester M. Hanson to Dr. Greene, the presentation of an enlarged photograph of the float to Aldro Hibbard and a host of after-dinner speakers, introduced by toastmaster Alvin S. Brown.

Some excerpts from the speech-making have more relevance to our story than others. In his initial comments, Toastmaster Brown claimed the honor of "finding" the Motif, which I would be remiss not to include. According to Mr. Brown, twenty-five years earlier (circa 1908), he himself "had taken

IMAGE 17. No awards were originally intended for the Best Parade Float, but officials changed their mind, and a Cook County official named Robert M. Switzer donated this one. Usually it sits on a shelf above the television on the second floor of the Legion Hall, along with five baseball trophies, but it was moved for this picture. *From the Trophy Collection of the Peterson American Legion Post, Rockport, Massachusetts (photographed by the author).*

a picture of the wharf, entering it in an amateur contest in Boston, where it won honorable mention under the title of 'Fishing Boats at Wharf.'"

Aldro Hibbard's comments that evening revealed candid feelings regarding Motif No. 1, which, in the ensuing years, he would be less likely to verbalize, gift horses being what they were to become. His comments, as paraphrased by the correspondent, follow:

> *Mr. Hibbard said that many do not see any reason for the popularity of Motif No. One. The building itself is not interesting, it is the conditions one sees the building under, plus what comes against it, such as the boats; otherwise, it would be commonplace. One artist, who happens to be painting the building, when asked what he would sell his painting for, said $100. The reply was, "why the building itself isn't worth that!"*[112]

We need not dwell on the diminishing of our fish shack by such an intimate observer as Aldro Hibbard, nor can we find fault in his argument.

The uninteresting structure would become interesting because of its fame and because of the ways it could benefit the town that Hibbard loved. Thus, Hibbard would come to play an integral part in nurturing and sustaining the visibility and importance of the shack, regardless of his opinion and the fact that he was not inclined to paint it much. For Hibbard, both a town leader and the *de facto* leader of the art colony, it was always about Rockport. And in fairness to Hibbard, the Motif was only at the beginning of its upward trajectory in the fall of 1933, and even he could not have predicted the prominence the fish house would ultimately achieve.

Over time, the good spirits and excitement would diminish. The parade was over, and in the morning, those in the hall would be back to their everyday lives and the challenges of those onerous economic days of the

IMAGE 18. This lone tin seagull may be all that's left of the famed American Legion parade float. *From the collection of the Sandy Bay Historical Society (photographed by the author).*

Great Depression. The float itself was destined for further showcasing, though under considerably less glamorous circumstances than its maiden voyage. Ultimately though, the wharf scene was removed from its chassis and sat on the old wharf beside the real thing for several years, gradually and inexorably consumed by the elements and souvenir seekers.[113] As far as I can find, a tin seagull in the collection of the Sandy Bay Historical Society may be the only bit of it that is left.

A CENTURY OF PROGRESS

When Somerville mayor Murphy spoke at the testimonial dinner, he commented that Motif No. 1 had also been called "the inevitable" because "an artist always did it sometime or other." Another part of his commentary bears some scrutiny. When elected to Somerville's mayorship, he reminisced, he had used the slogan "Modernize Somerville," but for Rockport, he said he recommended "Keep Rockport Ancient."[114]

Which brings us to the telling irony. The Chicago World's Fair of 1933, at which the American Legion Parade took place, bore the theme "A Century of Progress," a juxtaposition of the centennial of the city of Chicago with the progress of the physical sciences and their application to industry over the same hundred-year span. The message: Chicago had reflected, was continuing to reflect and was now about that kind of progress. The purpose of the fair of 1933, as it had been for the previous exposition in 1893, was to draw attention to the city, boast its success and status among other cities, generate revenue and stimulate investment for further growth.[115]

The struggling little town of Rockport, Massachusetts, shared these same goals. Because the year of the fair corresponded to the worst economic period in the country's history, the stakes were even higher and the effort even more pressing. In very different ways and by very different means—pursuing the same objectives in opposite directions, as it were—both Rockport and Chicago would accomplish their goals. Chicago succeeded in displaying the triumph of science and technology: an auto assembly line at the General Motors Building; an all-electric kitchen and central air conditioning in the House of Tomorrow; an extraordinary new invention in the Electricity Hall called the television.[116] Rockport succeeded by displaying a romanticized past of simpler times, when men "fought hard for life and livelihood"[117] with nets and traps, aided by the blessing of nature's winds billowing their sails and enabling a harvest from the seas. Chicago's salvation was in looking to the future, while Rockport's was in looking to the past—a past symbolized by an old fish house.

Chapter 6

Jack Buckley's Studio

The Good Soldier

It is obvious from the preceding pages that John M. Buckley deserves special attention in the chronicle of Motif No. 1. From 1931 to 1946—a period including much of the artistic zenith of both the shack and the art colony—Motif No. 1 was John Buckley's personal art studio. But more than that, Buckley, though overshadowed by Aldro Hibbard (who cast a long shadow in town), was arguably more important to the shack's fame and survival than any other individual. Without any doubt, Buckley was the "good foot soldier" of the Rockport art colony and contributed in unsung ways for over a quarter of a century. Still, his contributions to the town and the art colony, as well as his art, have been underrated—and here I hope to correct the record to some extent. (Plates 19 and 20)

Born in 1892 (the year Walter Wonson took possession of the shack on the old North Pier), Buckley was a relative latecomer to painting. The eldest of six from South Boston, Buckley was forced to quit school after eighth grade to help provide for his family after his father was killed in a construction accident. He joined the National Guard to supplement his income as a laborer and was subsequently called to serve as part of the 26th Yankee Division, which landed in St. Nazaire, France, on September 21, 1917.

Known by its veterans as the "Sacrifice Division," the 26th Division was in combat longer than any other American Division and sustained extensive casualties. Buckley, a sergeant in Company D of the 101st Infantry, was one of the wounded. During the Meuse-Argonne offensive, Buckley was not only

IMAGE 19. John M. Buckley
painting Motif No. 1.
Courtesy of John D. Buckley.

gassed but also took a bullet through the helmet, which grazed his skull above
his left ear before penetrating his shoulder, for which he received a Purple
Heart, as well as a recommendation for a Medal of Honor. He returned
stateside using a cane, with residual balance problems from his head injury.

Buckley was admitted as a "discharged soldier" to the Mass Normal
School of Art (now known as Massachusetts College of Art and Design)
on November 13, 1919, under a GI bill of sorts: as a "Special" student
sponsored by the Federal Board for Vocational Education. The twenty-
seven-year-old Buckley spent his first school vacation in 1920 as one of
Hibbard's initial batch of student veterans. After his sophomore year,
Buckley was again in Rockport, participating in the organizational meeting
of the Rockport Art Association and exhibiting in the inaugural show of the
Rockport Art Association.

Even in art school, Buckley evidenced a pattern of participation without
being top dog; he was less likely to be in the spotlight than in the role of the

trusty right-hand man. He was class treasurer both his junior and senior years and held the same office for the student government in 1922. He was advertising manager for *The Artgum*, the student publication, and served as assistant to Edward W.D. Hamilton, the legendary antique figure and composition instructor at the school, in "fixing up the electrical effects and caring for properties" for various school productions. We learn from the senior column of the graduation number of *The Artgum* that "he [Bucky] accepted all honors and served on every Committee that was ever appointed to the school!"[118]

During his junior year, Buckley married Marguerite C. Dooley, with eldest son John D. Buckley born in 1923 and second son Donald following six years later. Until 1928, when the family became yearlong Rockport residents, they occupied cramped summer quarters on the upper floor of 14 Dock Square, where Buckley ran an art supply store, the Rockport Art Shop, at street level. Although this art materials business doesn't appear in the Rockport Directory until 1925–26, Buckley likely began the business as early as 1921, if we are to rely on a 1927 brochure for Hibbard's "Rockport Summer School of Drawing and Painting." In it, Buckley is listed as business manager for the school, located at 14 Dock Square, where the Rockport Art Shop would "greet members of the Rockport Summer School just as heartily as it had greeted them for the past six years."

From another Hibbard school brochure, undated but possibly from as early as 1929, we learn that Buckley would be in charge of all the outdoor classes "as during the last two seasons," with Hibbard only conducting Saturday morning sessions of lectures and criticism. In the listing of this assistant instructor's credentials, we learn that Buckley had studied at the Rockport Summer School with Hibbard for five years (presumably managing the school concurrently) and had also been an assistant instructor at the Mass School of Art from 1923 to 1926, as well as instructor of freehand drawing at Malden Evening High School and instructor of drawing and painting at Boston University.[119] Perhaps as early as 1931, Buckley was no longer teaching for Hibbard but offering instruction on his own.

When Hibbard was elected president of the Rockport Art Association in 1927, his protégé Buckley was elected secretary, a post that he would hold until 1941, a year before Hibbard gave up his tenure as president. Whether performing in shows to raise funds for the March of Dimes or participating in Rockport Art Association events, Buckley was clearly at the ready to support his community in any way he could.

Jack Buckley's Studio

THAT FISHY SMELL IS TURPENTINE

In August 1931, Buckley portrayed a murderer in the opening number of a standing-room-only presentation of *Low Jinks* in the Rockport Art Association gallery and then led a cast of three pirates and a mermaid in *The Painter and the Pirate*. Set "near the familiar Motive No 1," Buckley played "an artist painting the motive under difficulties to be eventually captured by pirates. Next was shown the poor artist under the sea with new subjects to paint."[120] It was apropos that Buckley assumed the role of the painter of the Motif in the skit in 1931, since that very year he began leasing the shack from David Waddell and Motif No. 1 transitioned from fishery-related duties to a full-fledged art studio, as it would remain for the next fifteen years.

Prior to leasing and then purchasing the shack from Waddell, Buckley had been doing most of his painting outside, partly because he lacked working space above the art supply shop in Dock Square and certainly had no room to teach or display his own art. In addition to basing his teaching and painting in the Motif, Buckley used the space to make frames and stretch canvases, which he continued to sell along with paints and other art supplies. Unfortunately, and much to Buckley's consternation, a competing art supply store took his place in town after his relocation and ultimately led him to close up his own shop.

Buckley made his own improvements to the Motif, installing a kerosene stove, a sink and even a toilet at the two-story end. He also installed a dormer with a section of windows on the back side of the shack, allowing an opening for that all-important northern light. The second story was fitted with a bed and Spartan accommodations occasionally used by Jerry Fitzpatrick, a friend from Revere who was employed in procurement for the State of Massachusetts and stayed in the shack on holidays and weekends. For what it's worth, Fitzpatrick was the only person who actually slept in Motif No. 1—aside from perhaps the occasional anonymous alcohol-imbued lobsterman who didn't want to go home to face the wife.

As a valuable source of income in the '30s, Buckley was able to charge wharfage for Boston and Gloucester boats tying up at the wharf at a rate of $5.00 per month, $1.50 per week or $0.50 per night. For fishermen short of money, Buckley would waive the wharfage fees in exchange for fish or lobster to put on the dinner table. Prior to 1940, as many as ten boats could be tied up at the wharf at a time. Oldest son John recalls being ten years old and serving beer from a keg to fifty or so fishermen who were invited by Buckley to celebrate the end of Prohibition at the Motif. The beer was provided

IMAGE 20. A fishing boat tied up at the wharf, likely during the 1930s and John Buckley's tenure in the fish house. The two white signs on the two-story end of the shack are postings of wharfage fees. Note that the Motif could use some paint. *Courtesy of the Cape Ann Museum.*

in exchange for a fishing artifact of any kind—be it gaffs, hooks, oars or buoys—which Buckley hung on the inside walls of the shack. Olaf Norling, another veteran and lobsterman friend of Buckley's, would supplement the collection over the years by hustling additional fishing gear.

Buckley hung an unobtrusive sign on the Bradley Wharf end of the shack that declared the premises to be his personal studio and, in 1940, took out a half-page advertisement in the back pages of the *Artists of the Rockport Art Association*. Buckley's ad read:

> *Instruction in Drawing and Painting by John M. Buckley,*
> *Landscape Painting in Oils. Pencil Drawing A Specialty. Beginners Given*
> *Every Consideration.*
> *For particulars, write John M. Buckley. Motif No. 1. Rockport, Mass.*

THE HOME THIEME ADVANTAGE

If John Buckley owned Motif No. 1 in a literal sense, then Anthony Thieme certainly owned it in a figurative, or artistic, sense. Thieme, whom, like Hibbard, was one of the most famous and successful Rockport artists, was born in Rotterdam, Holland, in 1888 and moved to Rockport in 1929.

Without doubt, Thieme did more to publicize Motif No. 1—and thus the town—through both the quantity and quality of his artwork than any other single artist. Or, as the *Boston Globe* asserted, Thieme was "the first in the country to capitalize Rockport's now world-famous motif."

But how many times did Thieme really paint Motif No. 1? In the *Globe* interview from 1945, Thieme was quoted: "I paint it 200 times, maybe more. Sell every one. I paint it in the rain, snow, mist, fog, morning light, evening light…"[121]

As a comparison, Hibbard's daughter Elaine Clark estimates that her father—whose fame and reputation rested primarily on his winter landscapes of Vermont—painted the Motif altogether fewer than twenty times, and she could only specifically recall three paintings. In a feature on Cape Ann in 1949, *Holiday* claimed that Thieme had painted the Motif "nearly 400 times," and because he had "grossed more than $100,000 from sales on painting and reproductions," fellow artists referred to Motif No. 1 as "Thieme's gold mine."[122] How *Holiday* arrived at those figures we can only guess, as it perhaps did itself. In Thieme's obituary in the *Gloucester Times* five years later, the "some 400 times" estimate is repeated, as is the "gold mine" comment.[123] According to his obituary in the *New York Times*, Thieme reputedly earned more than $200,000 from all his artwork.[124] We can assume, though, based on the following, that the *Times* obituary writer had never been to Rockport: "A painter in both oil and watercolor, Mr. Thieme was well known for his landscapes, especially autumn scenes, and for his views of the picturesque in France, Spain, and Majorca. One of his best known works was 'Motif No. 1'—a view of a fish shack and wharf at Bearskin Neck at Rockport's summer art colony." A person relying solely on the *New York Times* might conclude that Thieme painted the shack only once, although that one painting was really pretty nice.

In any case, Thieme painted Motif No. 1 a lot, and any dispassionate observer can recognize a range in the quality of these paintings, not to mention a formulaic element. Regarding the issue of Motif No. 1 becoming an artistic cliché, one Cape Ann art collector assured me that the Motif remained a valid subject through Thieme's entire lifetime, if only through Thieme's stature as an artist. Essentially, when an art patron spent $1,500 on a Thieme painting in 1945, he or she wanted guests to see it hanging on the wall and know what it was. (Plates 21 and 22)

Perhaps the shack was becoming overexposed for everyone besides Thieme. One artist who studied with Buckley in the '40s suggested that young artists were intimidated by painting the Motif and being compared with the likes of the Dutchman. Another Rockport artist of the same era felt that the Motif had "been done, done, done, done…why should we paint it? But we did it." Clearly, if paintings of the Motif didn't sell, the Rockport artists would have been less inclined to continue painting it. The task was to find an interesting and fresh manner in which to approach the subject, and there is no shortage of examples of such explorations.

Thieme himself was not one to apologize for his financial success. Quoting from his 1945 interview: "Why shouldn't it [art] pay?" He [Thieme] demanded, "some unsuccessful artists call a successful artist 'commercial' just because his canvasses sell. They are only jealous because their own paintings have no market."

The Thieme School of Art, established in 1930, expanded such that, by 1940, the school included a new building with lockers, a dormitory on the grounds and an outdoor fireplace "for student's use," not to mention a "Large gallery for study of Mr. Thieme's works."[125]

Thieme's gallery complex was somewhat of a sensation, described by *Boston Globe* art critic A.J. Philpott as "probably the most ambitious thing of its kind ever undertaken by an artist in New England." Occupying a large parcel behind his house on South Street, the complex included a main gallery with "Roman gardens"—which initially showcased works by others—and two smaller galleries, one for his own paintings, and a third anteroom, which contained a fireplace, Chinese screens, sculpture, antique furniture and bric-a-brac. Besides this was the dormitory for students, Thieme's personal studio, a large garden and plenty of grazing room for farm animals. According to Philpott, Thieme was trying to solve the great problem of American artists at the time, which was the "problem of merchandising."[126]

On December 23, 1946, Thieme's showplace was destroyed in a two-alarm fire and reported as the lead story in the next day's *Boston Globe*. While Thieme and two of his workers managed to save as many paintings as they could, $15,000 worth of Motif reproductions were lost, along with reproductions of more than one hundred of his other paintings. The galleries were essentially a total loss, although the livestock was all saved and the student dormitory remained standing. Reportedly, more than thirty thousand summer visitors had inspected the galleries that previous summer.[127]

Thieme was known not only for the speed with which he painted but also for painting constantly. He modified his station wagon by cutting out the floor so he could stand and paint from inside it during inclement weather. Local Nick Mackey (whose father drove the parade float to Chicago and back) recalls seeing Thieme parked in front of the Congregational church, windshield wipers running, painting a street scene from inside his beach wagon.

Although Thieme and his wife Lillian "Becky" Becket often entertained Rockport artists at breakfast garden parties, most who were not part of his inner circle remember Thieme's aloofness. "Not one of the fellows," said John D. Buckley. "Not the sort who would be dancing in the studio [at Hibbard's parties] or playing ping-pong," said Elaine Hibbard Clark. And watercolorist Mary Robbins-Murphy related that one didn't "know" Thieme as much as "know who he was." If she happened to set her easel too close to where he was painting, he would "shoo her away."

If Thieme did "paint as if the devil possessed him,"[128] the demons within were not for outsiders to understand or pass judgment upon. Anthony Thieme fatally shot himself through the head at age sixty-six on December 7, 1954, in the bathroom in the Pickwick Arms Hotel in Greenwich, Connecticut, en route to his Florida home. Mrs. Thieme was in the hotel bedroom at the time, aware that her husband had been "suffering from a state of depression" but unaware that he even owned a gun.

TOUGH TIMES: RED SHACK AS GREENBACK

The years between 1929 and 1934 were extremely tough on Rockport artists, especially during the winter. For many painters, artwork became a necessary currency, with bartering a commonplace means of survival. Two of the medical men in town, Dr. Greene and Dr. Baker, had their office waiting rooms covered with local art (including images of the Motif, naturally) to attest to the fact.

Aldro Hibbard exchanged paintings to cover the medical expenses incurred in the births of both his children, and apparently other family medical and dental bills were paid in the same manner. Hibbard's daughter recalls eating a lot of oatmeal and creamed codfish with baked potatoes for dinner during those years, with milk coming from a neighbor's cow. A $1,000 art competition prize won by her father during this period "saved them that year." Later, in 1940, Hibbard swapped two large paintings for tuition deferral for his daughter at the Northampton School for Girls; apparently even when times had improved, he was more inclined to trade his paintings than lower his prices to sell them outright as bargains.

John Buckley was less dependent on bartering during the Depression because of his wharfage income and inside track to fresh fish but was generally less inclined to trade his art for commodities anyway. He also received a small war disability pension. Son John well remembers how tough those times were, with unpaved streets in the town and many townspeople wanting for food, clothing and coal. A perusal of the minutes of the meetings of the Board of Public Welfare during this period is sobering and confirms these recollections; one special meeting in particular was called to grant a citizen of the town a pair of shoes.[129] The town ran a "poor farm" on South Street, where people who had become destitute could obtain shelter and attempt to be part of a self-sustaining community.

The difficulties facing the artists in these times are reflected in this commentary by A.J. Philpott in his review of the Rockport exhibit presented less than two months before the Legion parade:

> The spirit of National Recovery permeates the artists who are represented…For in this exhibition—in various ways—the artists are trying to stimulate business and put some new life into the public taste for art. They are more conscious of the fact that artists generally have felt the effects of the depression in much the same way that cotton growers, farmers, and stock brokers have felt it in the past three years…There are some 1500 artists of one kind and another on Cape Ann this summer, and some of them are rather desperate. They say that unless the Government comes to their rescue, the way it has to farmers, cotton growers, and others, civilization may get a setback—in its culture and artistic task—from which it will not quickly recover.[130]

One consequence was the pricing of art. Philpott noted the absence of a "standard," with price variation dependent on how high a value the artists placed on themselves and their work. While he attributed the differences in valuation to "artistic temperament," I suspect that the differences were more dependent on "artistic financial straits."

For all intents and purposes, the hardest economic times for the artists in Rockport ended in 1935, owing to the impact of the Federal Art Project. Buckley participated in WPA programs as long as they were in existence, as did all the artists in town who could, with some switching from canvas to mural painting for public buildings. Paradoxically or not, art, music and dance all flourished in the '30s, and certainly the tough times on Cape Ann did not diminish the production or quality of the artwork. The *New York Times* reported on "Cape Anne's Thriving Art Industry" in the summer of 1936, noting that "the far-flung WPA [Works Progress Administration], preceded by the PWPA [Public Works Arts Program], has not, after all, done anything to jeopardize the output of private industry—at any rate, not on Cape Ann. What it has accomplished in the production line, is overplus, pure velvet."[131] And Philpott was equally upbeat in his coverage of the Rockport Art Association opening of that year:

> *And, make no mistake, there is a flock of artists and art students…from all over the country…also a great many literary and musical people, to say nothing of lawyers, doctors, architects, teachers and politicians who discuss the New Deal with the fishermen, granite cutters and psychiatrists.*
>
> *The artists and art student who haven't already painted, or made sketches of the old fish house on the end of one of the stone wharves on Bearskin Neck—known in art circles as "Motive No 1"—are busy doing so from every advantageous point of view.*[132]

Even if it curtailed purchasing habits, the Depression did not inhibit tourists from visiting Rockport in the summer to enjoy the scenery and the art, which was, after all, cheap entertainment. William Trayes, who grew up in Gloucester but summered in Rockport as a youth, remembers how he and his friends would count the number of New York and Massachusetts license plates to determine which tallied more. The Rockport Art Association drew crowds comparable to those of today, in large part due to the goings-on during exhibition weeks, in which Hibbard and Buckley, of course, always had a hand.

SELECTMAN CHARTRE PAINTS THE TOWN BLUE

If the Depression wasn't making things tough enough, seventeenth-century Puritans made matters worse through their contentious proxy, a retired U.S. Coast Guard commander and newly elected selectman by the name of Vincent Chartre. At a selectmen's meeting on July 8, 1937, Chartre proposed the strict enforcement of Blue Laws latent on the books, which prohibited businesses from operating on Sundays. The other two selectmen, though purportedly opposed to the ban, voted with Chartre, who defended his position both on the basis of his religious views as a devout Congregationalist ("It seems trite to say that there should be made some observance of the Lord's Day in any Christian community") and in the town's best interests ("the wrong class of people are attracted to the town, and…therefore property values in the community will depreciate"). More colorfully and provocatively, Chartre likened Main Street on a Sunday to the "cheapest honky-tonk in New England" and maintained that the town was slowly becoming "a miniature Revere Beach or Coney Island" and that a first-time visitor—expecting a quaint village of fishing shanties—would instead find himself in a "sucker's row" with "transient vendors."[133]

Officer Jimmy Quinn was obliged to notify the summer businesses the following Saturday and, after making his rounds the next day, reported that two gift shops and five galleries had violated the edict—including the galleries of Lester Hornby, Anthony Thieme, Otis Cook and the Rockport Art Association. Police Chief Sullivan dutifully proceeded to secure summons against all the violators. The seven defendants appeared in district court on July 15, and while hearings continued, artists and shopkeepers circulated petitions, the Board of Trade took sides with the artists and fishermen lost hundreds of dollars in Sunday sales.[134]

As the heated debate continued in person and in newsprint, Motif No. 1 was frequently invoked as a witness for the defense, standing testament that the artists in fact had "saved" the town. In a feature article, reporter Lawrence Dame of the *Boston Transcript* wrote:

> *"We can't do without the artists, and you can't make people religious by law," drawled one of the town's veteran fisherman, Capt. Billie Garrow, as he leaned on a rotting pile and looked across pungent fish nets and lobster pots at "Motif No. 1," the famous russet-colored old fish shed which has been painted more times than Rockport has years…"I remember when the first painters came here; I guess you could say we thought them freaks. Well, we know better now. They bring us a powerful lot of business, and I guess things would all shut up without them, now that fishing has got so bad and the granite quarries don't amount to much."*[135]

A.J. Philpott of the *Globe* asserted that artists and summer visitors had instilled new life, spirit and wealth in a town "which was more or less dead when the artists discovered the place, about 25 years ago," by extensively quoting an unnamed artist:

> *The artists have reclaimed Rockport and put it on the map in a big way. Its business—fish and granite—had practically vanished when the artists discovered its beauty and charm from a painter's point of view. They came and they painted, and in their train came the Summer visitors.*

Many of these visitors—and artists—bought houses or land on which they have built houses. They have improved and made livable old shacks and fish houses along the waterfront that had been abandoned…So that places that used to be an eyesore took on a sort of charm which the old fishermen never knew anything about—and don't yet understand.

Take for instance that old fish house out on the end of Bearskin Neck, which artists have been painting for a quarter of a century and are yet painting. That old building is known in the art world as "Motive No. 1."[136]

On Wednesday, July 21, Gloucester District Court judge Lincoln S. Simonds ruled that art museums and galleries could legally display paintings on Sunday but that it was still unlawful to sell art or offer it for sale, so shops needed to remain closed. Hornby, Cook and the Rockport Art Association were acquitted on lack of evidence, while Thieme, Arthur C. Smith (Bearskin Neck Art Gallery owner), Lewis Whitney (a pewter artist) and Miss Hale Anthony (proprietor of a "nautical gadgets shop" who had pleaded guilty) were all found guilty.[137] Thieme and Lewis appealed the ruling, and on October 29, Judge George F. James of the Salem Superior Court quashed complaints against both, effectively ending the matter.[138]

Enforcement of the ban would gradually disappear, resurfacing in the summer of 1961, when a statewide enforcement of Blue Laws temporarily came into effect until the rules were finally relaxed by statute in November of the following year.[139] But if Vincent Chartre had perhaps gone a bit overboard in resisting changes that were inevitable, one cannot argue that changes had come to Rockport. In a 1939 article written by Hibbard, the leader of the colony sounded a bit wistful.

"My first visit to Rockport around 1920, proved conclusively to me that the subject matter for a limited radius varied tremendously and that most of the material promised a life-long study regardless of indicative changes destined to take place with the approach of the speed age," he wrote. And although he still considered Rockport to be "perhaps the choicest painting and recreational ground on the Atlantic seaboard," he nonetheless felt "the necessity of precaution in any major development which may detract from or lesson [*sic*] the beauty of Rockport." The quarries were full of water but "still paintable." The greatest changes, though, had taken place in the harbor: "The fishing craft have largely discarded their canvas for motor power…Many of the fishing shacks have lost their original quaintness with the addition of porches and other features in being remodeled for summer residents. However, the general skyline is fortunately about the same."[140]

A.J. Philpott of the *Globe* was still accentuating the positive, noting that, despite its proximity to Gloucester, Rockport

> *attracts a greater variety of literary and artistic people than any of the other colonies on the North Shore. In point of fact, Rockport has been pretty much taken over by these people. It has lost its identity as a fishing port, and the granite industry which formerly flourished there is not very active. But it has retained its quaintness and homey charm.*[141]

And, naturally, he didn't forget to plug the old fish house on the end of the granite wharf, "which artists and students have been painting from different angles for many years." If all this mention is sounding repetitive, there were those who were beginning to feel that the shack's representation on canvas was becoming repetitive as well.

Of course, such heresy wouldn't be shouted out by the likes of A.J. Philpott. But we can offer into evidence a rather obscure publication called the *Cape Ann Log*, which was sponsoring an art competition for amateurs in the summer of 1939. All entries were welcome, with one caveat: "Rockport's motif number one, the only taboo in the Cape Ann Log's new sketching contest, has been so often reproduced that we offer it above in its sole appearance of the season. It's good but it has been said too many times before."[142]

Just an opinion. Anthony Thieme and others went on with business as usual. There were fish shacks and there were fish shacks, but Motif No. 1 was something special and was Rockport's very own.

Chapter 7

You Can't Judge a Cover by Its Book

We have seen that a fish shack does not become famous on its own. Civic bolsterers and countless brushstrokes on canvas can only do so much to ensure that attention does not stray. To stay on top, a shack needs a good PR person. Perhaps no single incident is more illustrative than a largely forgotten manufactured controversy, professionally and expertly exploited, that occurred in the summer of 1942, a time when the war was threatening to make a significant dent in tourism and local economies.

The precipitating event was Dial Press's unfortunate selection for the jacket cover of Mary Heaton Vorse's new book, *Time and the Town: A Provincetown Chronicle*. Labor rights activist, journalist and novelist, Mrs. Vorse had made her home in Provincetown, Massachusetts, for more than thirty years and had published an homage to the place and people of her adopted home. Katherine Woods wrote a glowing five-column book review in the *New York Times* on July 12, 1942, that was featured below a five-column halftone of the dust jacket, designed by illustrator Norman Reeves: a full frontal portrait of our hero, Motif No. 1, and Rockport Harbor.[143]

We can only speculate on how this admittedly non-earthshaking event transpired ("How about a nice generic New England harbor scene, Norm…"), although media reports of the time offer halfhearted explanations and rationalizations. A Provincetown book seller named Paul Smith declared that the jacket drawing was a composite picture, and while it included certain features of a Rockport scene known as Motif No. 1, there were dissimilarities, most notably that the wharf depicted was of timber construction rather than stone. In addition, "The steeple of the Provincetown Methodist

IMAGE 21. Norman Reeve's jacket cover for *Time and the Town*, by Mary Heaton Vorse, published in 1942 by Dial Press. *Collection of the author.*

Church is shown clearly in the jacket picture. The wharf in the drawing existed only in the illustrator's imagination."[144]

Echoing these sentiments, the author herself, who had approved the cover, simply declared, "I believed it to be a composite picture of Provincetown," seemingly unruffled. This, after all, was a woman who had been wounded by gunfire only five years earlier while covering the strike at the Republic Steel Corporation plant at Youngstown, Ohio.[145]

There is an additional irony here. In 1913, Mrs. Vorse and her second husband, Joseph O'Brien, had purchased a rickety old wharf in Provincetown, Lewis Wharf, with a fish house of its very own to use as their studio. Artistically notorious in its own right, this fish house became the "theatre on the wharf" for the nascent Provincetown Players. Mrs. Vorse's little fish shack, in fact, housed the premiere of Eugene O'Neil's first play, *Bound East for Cardiff*, which places it, along with Motif No. 1, in a very exclusive community of fish shacks. Unfortunately, Lewis Wharf collapsed in a winter storm in 1921, evidently resulting in a wharf/fish house shortage in Provincetown that resulted in the Motif assuming the identity of a shack from Cape Cod.[146]

Much of the verbal barrage hurled from the shores of Cape Ann was reported not just in the Boston and Cape Cod papers but to a national audience as well, including coverage of the kerfuffle in *Time* magazine.[147] Telegrams from Aldro Hibbard and John Buckley to the Dial Press started things off. Hibbard wrote:

I was shocked to the camel-hair bristles of my paintbrush to discover that you had used a drawing of Rockport's famous Motif Number One on the jacket of Mary Heaton Vorse's Provincetown book. We of the Rockport colony have always looked upon Provincetown as a weak sister in the family of art and this theft of our most sacred subject is a confession that the Cape Cod village is minus a house suitable to be reproduced in the excellent book of Mrs. Vorse.

Buckley wired: "Motif Number one is my personal studio. Therefore I join others in the Rockport colony in vigorous protest. In fact, I think I will see my lawyer."

Lewis Whitney, acting president of the Rockport Board of Trade and an artist who sculpted in pewter, wired the following to the Provincetown Board of Selectmen: "If Provincetown really needs Motif Number One in her weak struggle to keep on the artistic map we might present her with the replica which took first prize as a float in American Legion Parade, Chicago, 1932 [*sic*]."[148] And for good measure, Mrs. Anthony Thieme, who was not known around town as a "shrinking violet," allegedly also sent along a letter of protest.[149]

Not Just Whistling Dixie

The vehemence of these responses might seem disproportionate, but more to the point, these tirades are remarkably well crafted and too cute by half. There is an explanation for that. It appears that a man named Burton "Dixie" Johnston of Annisquam, a professional ringer, was a hands-on consultant.

Biographical details about Dixie Johnston are sparse, but John L. Cooley describes him as "a former Boston newsman, who had contributed several publicity gems to Hibbard's scrapbook."[150] Hibbard's daughter, Elaine Hibbard Clark, recalls Dixie from her childhood as a *Boston Herald* sports reporter, an ebullient man who would show up at their door and "bounce around." He sometimes had too much to drink, she recalls, and on those occasions when he did show up at the Hibbard household, he often smelled of whiskey. John M. Buckley's sons both remember Dixie as a flamboyant character often seen about town and similarly recall his fondness for imbibing. Nick Mackay, not mincing words, summed him up concisely as "a character and an alcoholic." Dixie also supplemented his income during the Depression by making and selling pralines in town. As an aside in a 1943 art exhibition review, A.J. Philpott makes casual mention of the man with "'Dixie' Johnston has added something to the gayety of the Neck [Bearskin Neck] with his little dining room."[151]

Hibbard, an accomplished baseball player who managed and played with the Rockport team for a number of years, enjoyed his associations with sports figures and ballplayers, which is where his interests intersected with Dixie's. A family guest book donated to the Sandy Bay Historical Society documents that Dixie attended a "Sports Night" held at the Hibbard studio on October 24, 1941; other invitees included former Major Leaguers Thomas J. "Buck" O'Brien (Red Sox roster in 1911–33) and Joe Dugan (Red Sox roster in 1922, Boston Braves player in 1929).

According to Cooley, Dixie Johnston "frequently collaborated—perhaps conspired is more accurate—in Al's [Hibbard's] baseball fortunes. Whenever they put their heads together, the sportswriters were assured of a good story under a Rockport dateline."[152] Johnston was as proficient in creating these "good stories" as Hibbard was a good sport in participating in them, and they successfully garnered sports publicity before and after the Vorse book incident. In May 1939, the pair had staged a painting lesson by Hibbard for the Cincinnati Reds' pitcher Johnny Vander Meer upon the latter's "discovery" that he was a descendant of the Dutch master Vermeer.[153] And in 1942, in response to the Rockport baseball team losing their first baseman Edward Roewer to the navy, Hibbard wrote a letter of appeal to Secretary of the Navy Frank Knox, requesting that the navy give them Cleveland Indians' pitching ace Bob Feller in exchange.[154]

In the case of the Vorse book cover, Dixie Johnston was able to demonstrate his talents outside of the sports realm. In response to the barrage of Rockport telegrams protesting the *Time and the Town* jacket cover, editor Burton Hoffman issued a public apology on behalf of the Dial Press on July 18, 1942, in which he admitted culpability but walked a fine line in trying not to further offend either of the towns: "The company hopes it hasn't offended the good people of Rockport by putting a Rockport scene on a Provincetown book, and also hopes it hasn't offended the good people of Provincetown."[155]

Unfortunately, the response as reported in Provincetown was less diplomatic. Taking the protest all too seriously, Provincetown opted for a more defensive and provocative course instead of defusing the situation with a shrug and good-natured chuckle. This choice, in fishing terms, was swallowing the bait whole.

The *Cape Cod Standard Times* coverage of July 18 included an interview with Brice McKain, director of the Provincetown Art Association, who admitted that the Dial Press had made an unfortunate mistake but contended that the situation was unimportant. Dismissing the matter and "returning to his palette and canvas," McKain was quoted, "If Rockport artists have nothing better to do with their time than to send letters and telegrams of protest to Mr. Vorse and to our selectmen, that is their affair." And if that wasn't petulant enough, consider the reaction of N. Edwin Lewis, chairman of the Provincetown Board of Selectmen, in response to receiving the telegram from the Rockport Board of Trade: "I feel it is a trivial matter," he said.[156]

Just *how* trivial was clarified by the *Boston Herald*'s page-two coverage of the story on the same day, expanding on Lewis's statement that the Provincetown selectmen had no reason to bother with the matter at a time when "they are engaged in wartime activities for the benefit of the town and all humanity."

> *Though outwardly presenting a brave front, the townfolk here today were mentally hanging their heads in humiliation at the chastisement inflicted yesterday by their artistic rivals, the people of Rockport.*
>
> *Lashed by Rockport because of the mistake in reproducing a Rockport scene on the jacket of a book dealing with Provincetown and its people, the folk of the town realize that, as one of them put it, "they haven't a leg to stand on."*[157]

The article concluded expectantly, nay, titillatingly, with: "But there was talk of drastic action." This, coming after the previous day's article that had concluded with, "They [referring to the indignant Buckley, Whitney and Hibbard] said that it was only the beginning."[158]

One might reasonably begin to suspect here that the *Boston Herald* was playing dummy to Dixie Johnston's ventriloquist, which would become increasingly evident over the ensuing week. The *Cape Cod Standard Times* would only manage a single comedic slap of its own during the entire episode. In its piece on July 18, it included a tongue-in-cheek quote from Captain Tally Crocker, identified as a "Provincetown lobsterman and patron of the arts," who, "aroused from a doze on the end of a genuine Provincetown wharf," responded to the flap with Rockport with, "Rockport? Never 'heerd' of it." From then on, Provincetown would take it on the chin, with the *Herald* engaging in the reportorial shooting of fish in a barrel.

This Is War!

Indeed, it was just the beginning. Along with the public apology, the Dial Press responded to Hibbard's wire personally with its own telegram: "Imagine our embarrassment. Our artist inadvertently did use Motif Number One. Is there anything we can do? Will you advise Buckley of this telegram? We are still blushing."[159]

Regarding the offer: "Is there anything we can do?" Not surprisingly there was, with Aldro Hibbard disclosing in the *Boston Herald* of July 21 that the publishers "had agreed to let a Rockport artist paint a Provincetown scene to replace the present one on the book."

That artist would be John M. Buckley, which the *Herald* reported in the following overstated manner:

> *And if that announcement* [a Rockport artist painting a Provincetown scene] *isn't enough to make blood run hot down Provincetown way, cast your eyes over this juicy detail. John M. Buckley, prominent artist and resident…has been selected by the publishers and a group of public-spirited citizens to spirit himself, by hook or crook, into the Cape colony to find a suitable scene for the new cover.*[160]

This was a story with legs, and it was milked over the course of an entire week, despite no shortage of hard news over the war in Europe and North Africa. While the battle was raging in Egypt and the Russians were pushing back the Nazis from the Volga, "irate Rockport commandos" were Provincetown-bound, the stage set "for a two-man commando raid on the sacred shores of Provincetown's art colony tomorrow morning by a well-known Rockport artist and a newspaperman." A little clam is whistling Dixie in my ear. Could that unidentified commando newspaperman by chance be one Dixie Johnston, embedded in his own story?

Motif No. 1, the cause of all the ruckus, was now apparently not only of artistic value but strategic military value as well. Said the *Herald*, "It was learned here tonight that friends of Buckley's fellow members of the State Guard have volunteered to watch over 'Motif No. 1' until his safe return from Provincetown is assured."

In essence, the *Herald* became the vehicle through which the merry band of Rockport artists could take pot shots at their defenseless art colony rival, the unwitting victims of a setup, brilliantly constructed by Dixie and friends. The *Herald* reported the "invasion" of Buckley—now referred to not only as a noted landscape and marine artist but also as a top sergeant in World War I—and set Provincetown up as the straight-town butt of jokes.

> *Asked what the new jacket for Mary Heaton Vorse's latest volume would portray, painter and ex-top sergeant Buckley remarked: "Typical*

Provincetown. It would never be mistaken for our Rockport."
    He had never visited here before, and said that his village, site of artists'
Motif No. 1 was a "paradise" compared to the Cape colony.[161]

The *Cape Cod Standard Times*, hamstrung, responded the next day as best it could, with fairly straight reporting until a bad sportsmanship dig at the end:

John M. Buckley, Rockport painter who owned a wharf known in Rockport as Motif No. 1, was in Provincetown today painting a picture of a Cape Cod pile wharf for the Dial Press. *Mr. Buckley's commission evolved from a controversy between Rockport and Provincetown art colonies over the jacket drawing…The Rockport artist declared that the drawing was made with his wharf as the subject. His claim has been substantiated by the publisher and one or two Provincetown painters.*
    Mr. Buckley's Provincetown painting will not be substituted by the publishers for the alleged Rockport drawing on the jacket. It was generally agreed locally that the commission was presented to him as a balm for his outraged feelings.[162]

The following day, the *Herald* continued its coverage, and by this juncture, journalistic license had morphed nearly completely into creative writing, with the piece stooping to the extent of the newspaperman quoting himself:

The sun was high in the heavens and the temperature hovered around 80 at Provincetown but the two Rockport commandos, who landed on its shores, had to wear their fur coats and mittens to shake off the chill of their reception. And they couldn't buy a cup of coffee to warm themselves…
    If the reception was cold, the next three or four hours were certainly hot. "Every truckdriver, or so-called artist, must have been specially commissioned as auxiliary patrolmen," Buckley said. "With every stroke of the brush we would have another 'patrolman' ask us for credentials and proper identification to allow us to stand on the wharf."
    "Why it got so hot that we had to join the Provincetown Art Association to continue our work," the other member of the two-party commando outfit declared. "Talk about unions. Why those 'artists' had us so tied up that they even made it impossible to buy a cup of coffee…"[163]

The reference to auxiliary patrolmen checking for proper ID was a sore point and, if not inaccurate, a punch below the belt, since the wartime restrictions could have a chilling effect on Provincetown tourism, if gas and tire rationing weren't bad enough already. Previously, the *Herald* had noted that Buckley had sketched under difficulty, as "military censorship was invoked on some of the wharves, forbidding him to glimpse Provincetown's expanse of limited sea" and obliging him to work with his back to the ocean.[164]

Thus the focus of a subsequent article in the *Provincetown Advocate*, in which readership was reassured that "taking of pictures anywhere in Provincetown, except any scenes which show the waterfront or any part of the coastal waters, will be permitted by visitors here."[165]

An Unexpected Ally

The episode does not quite end here, as a bombshell final volley was fired from a previously neutral camp. Gloucester artist Emile Gruppé surprisingly came to the defense of a Provincetown under siege and, in doing so, revealed a prickliness that bespoke the intensity of the rivalry among the neighboring artists. A Boston news story from August 6, 1942, revealed that Gruppé was irked by the fuss and that the reason the "Rockport coterie is so steamed up is that the Provincetown book jacket took practically the only subject in Rockport worth painting. They haven't anything else left. I don't blame them for protesting."

The tirade continued:

> *Rockport artists always come of* [sic] *Gloucester when they want to paint something worth while. Motif No. 1 is all right for students and tourists from the hinterland who don't know what real seafaring scenes are like, but the Rockport folks know very well that they couldn't get along without Gloucester near at hand to draw upon. Even with gasoline and tires scarce, the Rockporters clutter up Gloucester wharves. We're glad to have them in Gloucester, too. What I object to is the way the Rockport gang never lets on that it is dependent on Gloucester for art as well as fish.*

If that wasn't enough of a kick in the pants, Gruppé chastened the Rockport community for essentially breaking away from Gloucester for a second time in as many centuries: "If the Rockporters don't want to use the name Gloucester—they 'seceded' in 1840 and formed a separate town— let them sing the praises of Cape Ann, which embraces both Gloucester and Rockport."

And, concluding with the unthinkable: "What if something should happen to Jack Buckley's shack and there wasn't any Motif No. 1 anymore? The Rockport artists would be caught with their paints down."[166]

Aldro Hibbard patronizingly deflected the antagonism in the next day's *Herald*, making Gruppé come across as a man in bad straits who could do with some antidepressants, if not mandatory attendance at an "Aldro Hibbard's Anger Management Seminar." A portion of Hibbard's comments:

> *Gruppé's a very fine fellow, don't you know. Think the world of him. I suppose Gloucester has just got him down. You see, we've got all the business right here in Rockport.*
>
> *Poor old Gloucester. The town's as dead as a torpedoed whitefish. It's staggering along on its last legs and the only time it gets any attention is when we sent it some of the overflow crowds from Rockport. And Gruppé— he's an excellent fellow, really—has been quite despondent. We all feel for him, we really do.*[167]

Gruppé's contention that Motif No. 1 was the only thing worth painting in Rockport was, of course, an overstatement, but one can understand his frustration in Rockport so effectively hoarding the limelight. The Vorse incident reveals a publicity-savvy, and admittedly playful, group of artists in Rockport. But the funny business was serious. The business was tourism, and the rivalry among the art colonies was about more than art: it was about bringing in visitors from the outside to buy their artistic wares, among other things, and to divide the shrinking tourist pie to best advantage. Also at stake was the prestige of the colonies themselves. The relative latecomers in Rockport had clearly been on the ascendancy for some time, despite Gloucester's earlier cavalcade of more famous painters. In the 1942 Gloucester Directory, Gruppé was one of twenty-seven artists listed in the business section; by 1948–49, he was one of only nine, compared with thirty-seven listings for Rockport resident artists. Gruppé had seen it coming and didn't like what he saw, which certainly explains his irritation. Or perhaps he just needed a Dixie Johnston on his team.

Rockport artists consciously chose to consider themselves as such, rather than "sing the praises of Cape Ann." Any so-called Rockport School was less characterized by a specific, identifiable style than the fact that specific artists were associated more with the town of Rockport than any other—a town that was conspicuously linked to a commonly painted and photographed and very familiar red fish shack.

And thus the Vorse book jacket episode is but one of many efforts used to distinguish Rockport artists from the larger community of artists on Cape Ann. This establishment and preservation of a distinct identity—a brand, if you will—was the best means at hand for ensuring a competitive economic edge. Motif No. 1, the symbol of the brand, was used to full effect.

Chapter 8
THE COLOR RED

DADDY, WHY IS THE SKY BLUE AND THE MOTIF RED?

Until now, we have taken the Motif's color more or less for granted. But was it always painted red? Since red reads "dark" on orthochromatic film, return to Image 10, where we can compare our shack on Old Wharf with the white or gray shack on the end of T-Wharf. Motif No. 1 doesn't read all that dark.

We're on shaky, emulsive ground here. But the Motif definitely reads dark in a Martha Harvey photograph from the 1890s (Image 12). Perhaps the Motif was not painted red its first decade of life—instead treated with linseed oil or simply left to weather—but pigment had certainly been applied by the end of the century. And here I trust Harrison Cady and his watercolor of 1908; the opus *is* entitled *The Old RED Fish House*, after all.

So why red? Historically, oils such as linseed could be mixed with pigment derived from clay, flaxseed, cattle blood or plain old rust (ferrous oxide) to make a reddish color. According to marine historian Erik A.R. Ronnberg Jr., dories of the period were frequently painted with brick red, a concoction of brick dust, linseed oil and white or red lead used as a binder. Iron oxides for red paint were relatively cheap, so a shade of red was the most economical color if you weren't picky about the exact hue. The color choice for the Motif might have been someone's personal preference or perhaps merely a case of Yankee thrift.

Old-timers around Rockport don't remember our fish house in the '20s and '30s as red so much as heavily weathered with a reddish-brown tint. Recall that the WPA guidebook to Massachusetts, published in 1937, referred to a "little sail loft with a siding of vertical brown planks." Prior to 1940, in fact, the Motif was more often described as an "old fishing shack" than a "red fishing shack." And perusing the articles generated by the parade float of 1933, one can't help but note that the replica, at least, was not perceived first and foremost as "red," or in any case, the red color did not dominate its personality (as much as a shack can be said to possess one). In the years from 1896 to the '20s, the shack could have been painted any number of times with variations of red oxide pigment, but in all likelihood, there was more weathering than painting, and probably no painting at all.

Given this, I have suspected that the early Rockport colony artists played fast and loose with color and often painted the Motif redder than it was. Consider a Harry Vincent painting dating from between his arrival in Cape Ann in 1918 and his death in 1931. (Plate 11) Here we have a Motif boasting a substantial red color, but despite the boldness, the shack is still competing compositionally with the largest of the sloops and the strong verticals of the masts. A strong and exaggerated shade for the Motif is necessary to balance the intense colors of the water and boats, an artistic need that trumps any adherence to verisimilitude.

Next, consider two paintings by Anthony Thieme. (Plates 21 and 22) The first, from 1929, depicts a weathered gray shack without the least hint of red aside from the dot-like coloration in a couple of lobster buoys hanging from its side. The shack's absence of color is in keeping with the dull gray of the sky, water that appears brownish and turbid and a canvas that almost totally washes out into a haze of filtered light on its right side. In the second canvas, dating from 1935, after six more years of weathering in real time, the Motif is a definite and vivid barn red, despite the day being similarly gray and overcast. In all likelihood, the weather-beaten fish house wasn't much of an attention-getting red by then and would remain as such until its first major paint job, a good seven years away.

Now consider a watercolor by Gloucester artist Joseph Margulies from roughly the same time period as the later of the Thiemes. (Plate 23) The fish house is clearly no barn red but a washed-out brown. As testimony to the power of red, the focal point and star of the composition is not the Motif but a middle-aged lady art dabbler wearing a red hat and sweater in the left foreground. Of course, this watercolor is more about the art class than the Motif, but the piece may be a more accurate representation of the fish house color at the time than any other oil painting.

And this is where I walk out on a wharf, so to speak. I would argue that when exterior paint was finally slapped on the Motif for real (and predictably the colony made a big deal out of it), the chosen color was one that was more likely to have existed on the canvases of Rockport painters than a shade that had actually been seen or could be recalled by memory. A more cogent example of life imitating art is difficult to imagine.

Perhaps you think I have obsessed a bit much on the color red. Looking back to the beginning, though, I think it was the crankcase oil that really hooked me.

ALDRO'S SECRET FORMULA, OR THE CASE OF THE CRANKCASE OIL

Early in the course of my talking to locals, I encountered the enticing tidbit that Aldro Hibbard, while supervising a group of artists in the actual painting of the fish shack in the 1940s, mixed four gallons of crankcase oil into a red-tinted concoction. The reason for this, ostensibly, was to reduce glare, avoid a standard barn red color and maintain, as much as possible, the Motif's weathered look. In other words, the declared intention was to paint the shack and make it look as if it hadn't been painted at all. Not usually what the typical homeowner strives for with painting his or her house, but in this highly specific instance, perfect. And we're not talking about a standard paint crew carting around Sherwin-Williams cans and color-splattered ladders. Aldro Hibbard was a real painter and a fine one; if anyone could mix up a custom pre-weathered old red shack color, this was the guy.

I was captivated by the notion. Here was a beat-up aged shack that desperately needed painting, but a community of artists relied on its unchanged and appropriately weathered appearance for their artistic inclinations. A significant alteration of the Motif's hue was out of the question. Modification with shiny barn red paint—or, heaven forbid, fire engine red—would be nearly as egregious as installing green-and-white striped awnings to give it a cabana feel. So with Yankee ingenuity and the lofty goal of duplicating the forces of nature from a can, Aldro Hibbard devised a home brew with something cheap and readily at hand: crankcase oil. Brilliant.

Using crankcase oil to cut down the glare aspect seemed especially ingenious, something a creative and practical artist might think up (for the moment, forget about the existence of a non-glossy flat paint or stain, as I did). And so I imagined Aldro going to the local gasoline station and asking for four gallons of the stuff, and the station owner enthusiastically handing it over, saying, "I'll be glad to have you take it off my hands, Hib. I was just about to dump it in the harbor." This was a story not merely about art but about small-town resourcefulness, with the added bonus of making the world a cleaner place. I immediately decided that I needed to get my hands on that lost formula, to be forever known as the guy from Kansas who rediscovered the secret paint formula for Motif No. 1. Bragging rights were one thing; commercial possibilities were endless.

Of course, I was naïve. But in my defense, the crankcase oil story was widely accepted by those in the know around town. Specifically, when I asked a Rockport civic leader who was intimately involved with the rebuilding of the Motif in the '70s, he confidently replied, "Yeah, they did. They used crankcase oil," and then proceeded to substantiate his claim by informing me, somewhat less confidently, that he "had been told so by more than one person." An artist and former selectman told me that the crankcase oil "was used for its penetrating capabilities as well as mellowing." And a local historian not only accepted the story but also had reason to believe that the "secret" recipe had been locked in the town hall vaults. Of course, that was the "old" town hall, which had been razed, and who knew what had become of all that stuff in the vaults?

Shortly thereafter, I discovered a contemporary source for the story, a report from the *Boston Globe* dated August 28, 1942.[168] "In an effort to make sure that the red paint would not be too glaring," we learn, "Hibbard went uptown and got four gallons of crankcase oil to mix with the paint." But the key revelation comes one sentence earlier, where it is casually mentioned that "the paint job was organized by Dixie Johnston, local newspaperman."

A red flag in front of a red shack, if ever there were one. If Dixie Johnston had anything to do with feeding the story to the press, all was suspect. The context and timing of the paint job also gave one considerable pause, as the art colony painting project took place on the heels of Aldro, Dixie and Company's successful publicity coup over neighboring Provincetown over the Vorse book. This was more than shack maintenance; it was an encore performance.

And there was even more troubling evidence. At a subsequent similarly newsworthy "painting" of the Motif, this time in 1959, an Associated Press account reported that no painting had transpired for two decades, and despite having weathered to "a hue that stirs the soul of an artist," even the artists admitted that Motif No. 1 was "looking a bit shabby even for a fish house." Naturally, the paint had to look "'quiet' and 'weathered' enough to satisfy several hundred critical artists." A three-man watchdog committee, of which Hibbard was the artist member, asked for bids for the job and was reportedly shocked by the response: only one bidder asking seventy-five dollars to paint the Motif "red again."

The solution was suggested, according to the report, by a local oldster who rose at the meeting and exclaimed, "Heck, why waste paint, only the east side toward the ocean is down to bare wood!" In typical Yankee fashion, again, the town fathers slashed the painting cost to a quarter of the bid by voting to paint only "the side that faces Spain."[169]

The "yarn-like" colloquial quality of the reporting makes one question complete veracity, although the technique of painting only two sides of the shack at a time, separated by an interval of a year or two, was accepted practice on at least two occasions. But most disconcerting is the one sentence of the article that directly relates to the secret of the paint; specifically, that Aldro Hibbard "volunteered to mix a secret brew of venetian red, raw sienna, dashes of black and white, and shades known only to artists."

What? Secret brew? With no mention of the crankcase oil? How could Aldro leave out the crankcase oil? Depending on one's degree of skepticism, there are two choices here: 1) Aldro had forgotten his quip from seventeen years earlier and had come up with new quotable comedic material (i.e., the crankcase oil was a crank); or 2) the use of crankcase oil was now even more of a secret, too secret even to be mentioned for national security reasons (this was during the Cold War, after all).

THE QUESTION OF COLOR

One other significant point deserves mention that also escaped me at the time. No one in Rockport believes that the current color of Motif No. 1 approximates its coloration from its glory days or, more pertinently, from 1942 (nor from 1959, 1963 or even 1978, for that matter). Most locals who are old enough can remember for themselves, and anyone else only need peruse color photographs or postcards. But that doesn't necessarily mean that Hibbard's formula didn't exist somewhere. Maybe, I thought, there would be a reward for finding it so that the Motif could be returned to its 1942 authenticity.

As to the current color, I wasn't far from the mark when I opined earlier that the shack stands out like a sore red thumb. Many artists and old-timers are outright scornful of the current color, with one homegrown civic leader referring to it as "disgusting" and a prominent artist characterizing it as "denture pink." Another Rockport artist was more diplomatic when I broached the color question with him and patiently pointed out that even something painted red isn't entirely red. Specifically, he drew my attention to a painting in his studio and the use of the color green in the depiction of a red object. Perceived color depends on light and shadow, weather conditions and time of day, I was informed. Besides, most art is not merely representational but expressionistic.

I nodded to convey my comprehension. Of course, not that many artists paint the shack nowadays anyway, but his points were all well taken, the subtext being that the artist can make the shack any color he or she damn well pleases.

In Which the Naïve Narrator Is Foiled, but Not for Lack of Trying

I spent considerable time ruminating on the color red and the secret formula. I even went to the extent of obtaining a salvaged sample of the original shack and sending it to a historic restoration company for paint analysis. I actually told my point person at Building Conservation Associates, Inc., in Dedham, Massachusetts, to be on the lookout for crankcase oil residue (which, to be candid, I now find much more embarrassing than my earlier confusion of the two breakwaters). Samples were embedded in clear polyester resin cubes, and cross sections were viewed at high magnifications in both visible and ultraviolet light using Nikon SMZ-U and Nikon Labophot microscopes, the latter with magnification power of up to five hundred times.

My samples were soon thereafter returned. To summarize the findings: totally inconclusive. The Motif scraps were simply too weathered for analysis. Of all the luck, my pieces were likely from the side that faced Spain.

In Which the Narrator, in Desperation, Resorts to Enhanced Interrogation Techniques

While waiting for the results of the paint analysis, I arranged an interview with three town employees at the center of the care and feeding of the Motif. My meeting was in the basement of town hall with then Rockport director for public works John Tomasz; George Robertson, at the time field coordinator for the Rockport Public Works Department; and Jack Monroe, building maintenance foreman for the Town of Rockport. Rockport colony artists were displayed prominently on the walls of town hall, as they are in all public buildings in Rockport, and appropriately enough, a W. Lester Stevens painting of Motif No. 1 loomed directly above my head. On the surface, I was seeking pertinent nitty-gritty details of the present maintenance of the town treasure, but my hidden agenda was more sinister: to weasel from these town employees the secret glare-reducing paint formula, the unique mixture of tints and extraneous compounds devised by Aldro Hibbard.

I waited patiently for a good opening to bring up the question of the paint formula. I learned, among other things, about the new roof put on the Motif fairly recently at a cost of $14,000. I learned that the windows of the Motif had to be replaced relatively frequently because of the exposure and harsh conditions at the site. I learned that Jack had built a storage shed for the harbormaster on Granite Pier in 2000 that was an exact miniature replica of the Motif, based on the 1966 plans sketched out by the previous director of public works, Spaulding "Salty" Owens.

And then I learned that the place we'd been talking about had been painted by the Rotary Club about a year or so previously. We had drifted to the subject of paint, and I saw my opening.

Deeming a straightforward approach the best, I looked Jack Monroe directly in the eye and asked: "So what's the secret paint formula?" adding quickly, "Do they still use the crankcase oil?"

I was striving for an impression that I might already know the secret formula and simply was inquiring if they were using the same one. I reasoned thusly: if I already knew a secret formula and just wasn't sure if they were using the same formula or a new, improved one, Jack wouldn't be violating any sacred oaths or town regulations if he spilled the beans. Jack seemed like a nice guy, and I was just trying to get him off the hook. In theory.

"In the old days," he said, "in about 1900 to 1910, they used to use cow's blood to make red paint."

I wasn't sure if Jack was obfuscating or giving me a clue. If the latter were true, things were getting mighty interesting. A base of venetian red, some crankcase oil, a couple chalices of cow's blood—what else? I wanted to know exactly.

"So what's the formula?" I pressed on.

"If I tell you," Jack said, "then I'll have to kill you."

"Aw, come on…"

I waited, and Jack finally said it.

"Cabot's Barn Red."

I don't know how much time passed, but eventually I responded. Enough time had passed, at least, that the three of them realized I had been serious. I was stunned, and the only thoughts I could muster related to confirmation that there had been no necessity of me wearing a wire to the meeting.

"Cabot's Barn Red," I said. "The secret paint formula for Motif No. 1 is Cabot's Barn Red."

"Right," confirmed Jack. "Latex."

"Latex Cabot's Barn Red."

"That's right."

The three men, at some level, sensed my profound disappointment. In retrospect, I don't think any of them had heard about Aldro's secret paint formula before our meeting.

"I think they may have used an oil stain prior to 1978," George piped in, sensing the meeting had gone sour and conversationally attempting to get past it. "I think I remember something about old cans of oil stain being found in 1978…"

I was inconsolable.

To make matters worse, after consulting Joe Mitchell, owner of Ben's Wallpaper and Paint in downtown Gloucester, I learned that the formula for Cabot's Barn Red Paint had been recently reformulated. The revised recipe—which currently covers the Motif—includes the appropriate amalgamation of blue, red oxide, white and magenta but is missing the black pigment present in the original version.

So, adding insult to injury, the town had purchased an altered, non-black pigment-containing version of the stock barn red color. Even I, a non-artist, could tell that the current color needed a splash of black, if not a generous dollop of crankcase oil. In any case, with the paint can pretty much closed on the present-day color, we can venture back to August 1942 to try to resolve the question of Hibbard's crankcase oil.

THE REST OF THE PAINT JOB STORY

The tempest over the Mary Heaten Vorse book jacket cover had pretty much spent itself by the last week of July 1942, although the post-battle parting shots exchanged between Hibbard and Emile Gruppé carried over to the end of the first week of August. The unanticipated success of that venture had undoubtedly inspired continued publicity efforts. The iron was still hot, and Dixie Johnston, Aldro Hibbard and John Buckley knew they needn't wait for serendipity to drop another golden egg into their laps; why wait for the right pitch when they could toss a sweet one to themselves?

Thanks to a Nazi tank wedge being wiped out at Stalingrad and the Russians bombing Berlin, the story on the shack's painting was buried on pages eight and thirteen of the *Boston Globe* and the *Boston Herald*, respectively. Still, the news made it to the wire services, which was likely the primary goal. Tellingly, the painting of the shack didn't even make the *Gloucester Daily Times*; the staged refurbishing of the Motif was clearly not intended for the locals.

So, on the morning of August 27, 1942, a group of Rockport artists marched to the Motif, led by none other than town patrolman Jimmy Quinn, a man not lacking in escorting expertise, as we know. John Cooley provides a pertinent detail not included in news reports of the time; namely, that "they were accompanied by eager photographers and correspondents."[170] Obviously, Dixie Johnston had been successful in getting the word out to his friends and colleagues in the news business.

As chronicled in the 1942 *Boston Globe* article:

> *Rockport's world-famous fish shed at the edge of a wharf, which has been the subject of more sketches and paintings than any other shed in the world—received a new coat of red paint this afternoon from the loving hands of the Rockport artists.*
>
> *Fearing that the weather-beaten 75-year-old shed might rot away if it were not painted and unwilling to trust the famous art class subject to a house painter, some 40 artists not only volunteered their services but even paid $1.50 a piece for the privilege of applying an antique red finish to the structure.*

For an added bit of theater (and perhaps to enhance the charade), John Buckley was not among the marchers. He was in his studio that morning, reportedly caught by total surprise when the horde of marchers, brushes and paint cans in hand, knocked on his door. According to the *Globe*, the artists "calmly told the owner of the building, John M. Buckley, also an artist, who had his studio there, that they had come to paint Motif No. 1. It was news to Buckley, but he made no objection."

Cooley presents the story with more embellishments in his two accounts. According to *Rockport Sketchbook*, after being told that the artists had come to redecorate his premises, Buckley allegedly said, "That's news to me, but why should I make a fuss? Go right ahead—and thanks very much." In the account from Cooley's biography of Hibbard, the latter allegedly told Buckley that he hoped he (Buckley) didn't mind red, to which Buckley reportedly replied: "Well, there isn't much color on the poor thing now, so go ahead."

The *Sketchbook* also reproduces a photograph of twenty-seven artists/ painters (not the reported forty; rounding up suspected) posing in front of Buckley's shack. By the looks of the scattered three-piece suits and Sunday dresses among the crowd, not everyone intended to stay past the photo op. Nonetheless, all of the artists did stick around long enough to observe the mixing of the paint so that the final shade of red met their endorsement. "Our objective was to keep away from the fire engine red. We believe we've been successful, but like a lot of other things we shall have to wait to be sure," said Hibbard when the job was done.

BACK TO THE CRANK CASE

That was the last we ever hear of the crankcase oil. Later on, however, the painting of the Motif still managed to break into the news, with media reporting additional paint jobs in May 1959 (only the ocean side painted, as noted above) and May 1963 (only two sides painted, the remaining two left to await another year).[171] Not surprisingly, Aldro Hibbard was still advising the workers on how to mix the paints. The staged theatrical elements were lacking, though, maybe because Dixie Johnston was no longer around (he has disappeared from the Rockport Directory by this point) or, more likely, because Hibbard didn't think he needed to promote more tourism; the Motif was famous enough. Hibbard had died by 1976, when the Motif was scheduled for another repainting, but artist William Flynn was recruited for professional advice about the proper paint color. I asked him about the formula in a phone interview.

"I reasoned," Flynn told me, "that Hibbard would be an old Yankee who would probably have a little extra paint in the house, and down in the [Hibbard's] cellar we discovered a can of [Martin] Senour paints, barn red, simple as that."

This circumstantial evidence of the paint can in Hibbard's basement, of course, has no real bearing on the crankcase oil issue, since the leftover paint, if even used for the Motif, likely would have been from the more recent paint jobs. At the time, though, the *Boston Globe* reported that Flynn could "now mix the paint to match the color in the can."[172]

The Color Red

From what I was told, no skill-dependent mixing and matching was involved. On the basis of his discovery, Flynn recommended oil-based Martin Senour paint, Barn Red, to the folks at J. Raymond Smith Hardware. But as the local hardware concern had switched paint stock, they substituted the Barn Red manufactured by Cabot. What the Rotarians slapped on Motif No. 1, provided by the town's Public Works Department, didn't much matter anymore, anyway. As long as it was red, of course.

But Flynn proceeded to inform me that he always used crankcase oil, mixed with turpentine, for the inside of his wooden gutters. Joe Mitchell at Ben's Paints in Gloucester confirmed this practice, although a mixture of linseed oil and turpentine is more often used. Mitchell also told me that shortly after World War II, an old-time painter he knew in Michigan would go to all the nearby gasoline stations and collect used crankcase oil, which he would mix with paint thinner or turpentine and color with lampblack tint or iron oxide pigment. Certainly one way to cut back on paint costs, although the blend would take a month or so to dry and might still be tacky six months after application.

"So do you believe that Hibbard actually might have used four gallons of crankcase oil?" I asked him wearily.

"I can believe it," said Joe.

And so can I, I suppose, although I also can believe that "four gallons of crankcase oil" made good copy for the dispatches sent to the press outlets by Dixie. All the better that it was plausible. Maybe Hibbard had mixed in some lampblack along with linseed oil—anything to keep away from that old barn red.

Chapter 9

THE TOWN SHACK

FISH SHACK FOR SALE

At the time when Buckley's studio was receiving its fresh coat of paint in late August 1942, the artists throughout Cape Ann were "working largely for the future when war will have ceased and the world gets back to… normalcy."[173] Before that normalcy could arrive, however, John Buckley put Motif No. 1 up for sale.

Article 39 of Rockport's Annual Town Meeting Warrant for Monday, March 5, 1945, reads: "To see if the town will vote to raise and appropriate a sum of money to purchase the wharf, and the building thereon known as Motif #1, or to acquire an option for the purchase of the same, or to take any other action in regard to acquiring said property for public purposes and preservation of said building. Inserted by petition."

Though Buckley admitted to a great love for the wharf and a great interest in the building, he later explained his reasons for selling: "I took a position out of town and so had no further use for the building. I had a chance to sell it and was told the town was interested in it and I was interested in having the town obtain it. I only hope that the character of the building is not altered in any way."[174]

Lobsterman Bill Donovan—a repository of local oral history—had been told that Buckley offered to sell the Motif for $3,000 to a group of fishermen, including harbormaster Tony Contrino, in the late 1930s. At that point, Buckley had moved his family to a larger house at 5 Atlantic Avenue, was no longer selling art supplies and primarily taught painting outdoors. Perhaps the Motif was a luxury he could no longer afford.

Certainly by the mid-1940s, Buckley's ownership of the studio had become a financial burden. Sometime during the war, he had taken a job as a middle school art teacher in Natick, in addition to teaching evenings at the Cambridge Adult Education Center. During the week, he rented a room in Natick and only returned home for weekends (when, on Sundays, he could take on private students during the winter). In addition to financial concerns, Buckley had developed arthritis in his hands, which made it increasingly difficult, and eventually impossible, for him to paint.

Obviously, the Town of Rockport needed to control the wharf and Motif No. 1; the idea of a private purchaser developing the property and not preserving the building in its current state was unthinkable. Buckley preferred to have the town make the purchase than sell to anyone else, even at a financial cost to himself.

Discussion of the town purchase of the Motif took place on March 6, 1945, the second night of the town meeting. Considerations included the potential use of the wharf and shack (possibly as a town landing, a fisherman's memorial or waterfront storage), plus the question of who would be in charge of it (Park Commission versus selectmen). Town attorney Sumner Y. Wheeler promptly threw cold seawater over the whole idea by informing the gathering that the town could not take any land for public purposes without defining its exact nature; a memorial for fishermen would hardly qualify. Moreover, Wheeler told the sponsors of the article that he thought it was drawn illegally. A motion to delay until a new article could be drawn up was defeated. Finally, a solution acceptable to the town attorney was proposed—namely, the use of the purchase as a memorial to the five hundred local men in the armed forces.[175]

The approximately 185 persons still present at the meeting unanimously passed an amended motion, and Motif No. 1 became property of the Town of Rockport and an official war memorial.

RED SHACK, REDDER TAPE

The *Boston Traveler* reported, "Buckley was congratulated for setting the price at a figure considered reasonable in view of the commercial possibilities of the building."[176] No good deed going unpunished, however, the transaction had still not been completed by October 25, 1945. Evidently, the town could not proceed with the purchase until the state legislature took action, and the delay meant that Buckley was responsible for accrued mortgage interest of

$66.[177] The selectmen received a letter from Director of Accounts Theodore N. Waddell regarding the dilemma of the interest and his professional opinion: "Unfortunately the wording of the act restricted the amount that could be paid for the land to $3600, which, of course was the amount the town had voted to pay for it. Regardless of how we might feel as to the reasons for the request, I do not believe under Chapt. 551 that he [Buckley] could be paid more than $3600."[178]

An accrued interest of sixty-six dollars standing in the way, the money had to be raised somehow. And apparently it was, in some fashion, as the selectmen meeting minutes record that the "Board approved Town Attorney and Town Treasurer's acts in settling property of John M. Buckley's so called Motif No. 1." They also voted to appoint Buckley as caretaker beginning on November 23, 1945. Of course, nearly eight months earlier, and a little over a week after the town approval for the purchase at the town meeting, Buckley had requested the selectmen's permission to occupy Motif No. 1 as a tenant, a request that had been "laid on the table." [179]

On March 28, 1946, J. Eugene Sullivan petitioned the selectmen for use of "Bradley Wharf and building known as Motif No. 1" for storing lobster gear and was informed that a five-man committee regarding use was to meet and make recommendations, with their initial meeting scheduled for April 2. On June 13, 1946, the board discussed the possibility of wharfage charges at their recently acquired town property, but on the advice of Town Attorney Wheeler, the matter was dropped in view of "the accident liability situation."[180]

And thus matters stood until February 13, 1947, when the selectmen meeting minutes record that:

> *George Soini, Pearl King, and Steve Orr appeared to see what could be done for them as Mr. Wright* [the John B. Wright Fish Company of Gloucester owned Hodgkin's Fish House on New Wharf as well as a shack on the end of T-Wharf] *had ordered them either to deliver lobsters to him or get out of his shacks. For this reason, the Board of Selectmen voted to let them have Motif No. 1.*[181]

The back story here is not entirely clear, but I would assume that the selectmen took pity on three well-liked lobstermen, about to become shackless owing to landlord troubles, and decided to ignore liability issues, if there were any. Maybe Town Attorney Wheeler wasn't around that day, or perhaps the lobstermen were simply persuasive: Pearl King was described as "one of the toughest sonsabitches on the Neck."[182] But the consensus at the time of town purchase had been that the fish house should be available for the fishermen after all, so despite town bureaucracy, Motif No. 1 returned to a maritime role, though scaled back from its fishery glory days. For painters, of course, the shack was still just a façade, its beauty only plank deep, a rare and notable exception being a depiction of the Motif on the inside, painted in 1955 by Gunner Bjareby. (Plate 24)

THE RETURN OF THE LOBSTERMEN

Bill Donovan, who hauled bait as a kid for longtime Motif-based lobsterman Yuk Mackey and began lobstering himself in 1957–58, was using a stall in Motif No. 1 when it was destroyed in 1978. Luckily for him, his current lobster shack on Bradley Wharf (which he purchased in 1983) was vacant at the time and available for lease. Now retired, he continues to make lobster traps and buoys the old-fashioned way—that is, from wood. His handiwork is authentic but purely decorative and no longer sea-bound, since these days lobster traps are made of wire and buoys of Styrofoam. Wooden lobster buoys began leaving the scene in 1970 and became illegal by Massachusetts state statute in 1974, since they can cause damage to propellers and fiberglass boat bottoms and are considered a menace to navigation. Most of the old wooden buoys used by the lobstermen in Rockport were taken to the dump or burned.

Which brings us to the decorative wood buoys on the front side of Motif No. 1, which prompt visitors to describe the Motif as a "lobster shack," a not entirely accurate characterization. As objects, buoys automatically convey a marine narrative, but they also reveal the more specific history of an individual lobsterman by their color schemes. In 1974, just as wooden buoys were banned by the legislature, the Board of Selectmen decided that hanging the buoys of old-time Rockport lobstermen on the outside of Motif No. 1 "would be picturesque and a good way to honor lobstermen."[183] An active and conservation-minded citizen named John Burbank—who had occupied the upstairs space of the Motif since 1968—took responsibility for collecting old buoys and bolting them on the shack.

The relevant point is that wood buoys needed to be changed out twice a year and hung out to dry for a couple of months, while Styrofoam ones don't; hence, the "real" working buoys, functional as well as picturesque, that appeared on the Motif after 1947 were gone after 1974, when "display" buoys were substituted. Between 1931 and 1946, when Motif No. 1 functioned as John Buckley's art studio, no buoys hung on the fish house exterior walls, and hence they are absent from paintings and photographs from this period (note that there are buoys in the 1929 Thieme painting, Plate 21). Conversely, photographs and paintings from the '50s and '60s frequently reveal large numbers of buoys hanging on the front side of the Motif, most notably the red and white ones that belonged to George Soine, a hardworking lobsterman and one of the first occupants of the shack upon its return to a fishing function. (See Image 24 and Plate 28, and note the absence of buoys in Image 23)

Motif No. 1 Gets Its Day

The official dedication of Motif No. 1 did not occur until May 14, 1950, when an estimated 350 people endured "simple but impressive exercises" that ended with the unveiling of a wall plaque by Board of Selectmen chairman Ernest R. Poole Jr. Along with land-bound spectators, newsmen and the American Legion Band, the scene included festively decorated U.S. Coast Guard boats at anchor and two docked Italian fishing draggers. Adding to the colorful surroundings were Coast Guard flags "strung from the building along the wharf, spelling out in the language of the flags, the words 'Motif No. 1.'" More on those flags later.

We can now heed some of the words of the principal speaker of the day, Selectman William P.C. Smith:

> Probably I don't appreciate what the artists see in it but I have a painting of it done by Aldro T. Hibbard and I do appreciate that. I feel that Motif No. 1 is the symbol of Rockport. It really is Rockport. It is one medium of advertising that has advertised Rockport more than any other. You see it in the newspapers, the magazines, the movies, all over the country, across the pond and in South America. We owe one group a lot, the least appreciated group, the artists.[184]

It was official—Motif No. 1 was now "the symbol of Rockport." In the context of defining it as "a medium of advertising," though, Smith demonstrated a coldblooded business practicality. Subtext here for the cynics among us: "Thank you, artists. You know how to paint, but we know how

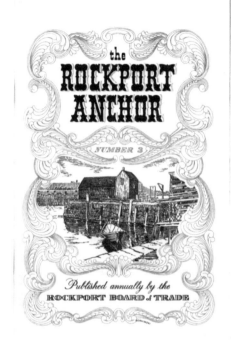

IMAGE 22. *Rockport Anchor* covers from 1952 (left) and 1958 (right). *Courtesy of the Cape Ann Museum.*

to promote our town. The Motif is ours [insert sinister laugh here]." With the Motif firmly in place as the town's icon, the Board of Trade promptly launched an ambitious promotional pamphlet called *The Rockport Anchor*, which featured Motif No. 1 on the overwhelming majority of its covers until publication ceased in 1999.

But about those flags. About two weeks before the planned dedication, artists noticed in horror that three new wires, hanging in one-hundred-foot arcs "like clothes lines," had been strung from the shack to supply electricity to the pump for the saltwater lobster pool belonging to Dana Vibert, who ran the Roy Moore Lobster Company (a couple less obtrusive wires had been in place for years, although you wouldn't know that from most of the press accounts).[185] Apparently, Mr. Vibert had requested permission to install the lines, and the selectmen had given approval at a time when watchdog Aldro Hibbard was away painting in Vermont. The protests—including those of Hibbard, whose heartfelt supplications referred to the Motif as a "sacred monument" that the town had purchased precisely so it would "remain undesecrated by power lines and other things"—fell on deaf ears. Selectmen chairman Poole, defending the decision, stated: "The selectmen are just trying to be fair. We can't help keeping in mind that if anyone moves a lobster pot or a dory or anything else at the Motif, there's a protest. Well, if the fishermen aren't allowed to use the place, they'll move everything away and the artists wouldn't like that."[186]

Dana Vibert came up with his own defense: "If you don't like the wires, don't paint 'em."[187]

But what about the photographers who were coming from far and wide to take photos of the new "symbol," now marred by the unsightly wires? For the dedication ceremony, at least, the town had a cunning plan, or at least a quick one-day fix: the old U.S. Coast Guard flag camouflage gambit.

The need to avoid such conflicts in the future was recognized and prompted the formation of a three-person Motif No. 1 Committee. Charter members were the two principals in the wire wars, Aldro Hibbard, representing the artists, and Dana Vibert, representing the fishermen, with Frank W. Tarr serving as a tiebreaker, a civic leader impartial to brush or bait. A subscription drive was initiated in the meantime, with $100 raised for the noble cause of burying the wires. Instead of paying for contractors, a group of artists dug the trench themselves, saving a few bucks and creating some good publicity, until all was ready for the actual wire cutting: the centerpiece of the second annual Motif No. 1 Day festivities.

We can sense the beginning of shifting tides for the *raison d'être* of our shack, "with an exciting round of events planned by the Rockport Board of Trade for the expected tourists and summer friends of Rockport and Pigeon Cove." The purpose of the "big day," we learn from page one of the *Gloucester Daily Times* of May 24, 1951, was "to convince summer visitors that Rockport can be most alluring much earlier in the year than is usually the time for the influx of people and to honor the old fish shed that has won Rockport national prominence."[188]

Six hundred persons reportedly enjoyed the pageant in Dock Square, which included a costumed reenactment of the town's history, before proceeding to Bradley Wharf for the ceremonial cutting of the electric wires. This task was assigned to the chairman of public safety, who performed it somewhat warily, though reassured by a representative of the Gloucester Electric Company that his actions would not result in electrocution. Each snip of a wire was accompanied by a booming drum and trumpet fanfare, courtesy of a Rockport High School band sextet. But I am most intrigued by a symbolic representation of the "lament about the wires and what they had done to the Cape's state of mind" that occurred immediately before the wire cutting:

> *To pictorialize the sentiments* [as they were narrated by Master of Ceremonies Thomas C. Dolan, suitably attired in a top hat and cut-away tails]…*two young ladies, Joyce LaFlam and Moisha Kubinyi, gave an interpretative dance, containing disdainful steps and pointing at the wires, and climaxed by their divesting outer garments to expose fetching bathing suits, and into the waters of the frigid harbor, they dove in what was apparently their effort to escape from the sight of the wires. They swam to a neighboring wharf. The girls were on the program as the spirit of Cape Ann protesting the presence of the wires.*[189]

By the fifth annual Motif No. 1 Day—which had a Gay Nineties theme and featured Lester Hornby dressed as an early nineteenth-century English sailor and the "rediscovery of Motiff No. 1"—an estimated four thousand persons from all over New England were swarming "through its [Rockport's] narrow twisting streets and out onto its fishing piers from early morning until late tonight."[190] The tradition of wearing period costumes for the day would gradually die out in the early '60s, but Motif No. 1 Day, scheduled the weekend before Memorial Day, continued to inaugurate the summer tourist season.

THE TIMES, THEY ARE A'CHANGING

The fact that both the first Motif No. 1 Day and the inaugural publication of the *Rockport Anchor* occurred in 1950 was no coincidence. The town had owned the Motif for nearly four years, and certainly the dedication delay wasn't due to a four-year waiting list for the production of bronze shack plaques. The timing of both the special day and the uber-brochure was the brainchild of the Rockport Board of Trade as a response to the changing dynamic of tourism. The automobile had come into play in the '20s and '30s, but the day-tripper had only been one type of tourist coming to town, with most staying for longer periods of time in boardinghouses or hotels in Pigeon Cove. With the completion of Route 128, a circumferential highway connecting Cape Cod to Cape Ann, the day tourist was now overwhelmingly dominating the scene. In August 1950, the last section of the 860-foot A. Piatt

Andrew Bridge was set in place over the Annisquam River as an alternative to the low-level Richard Blynman Bridge to the east that produced massive traffic backups due to its frequent opening.[191] The Rockport Board of Trade simply needed to give the visitors a reason to pass through Gloucester and come directly to Rockport.

Their efforts clearly were successful, if only measured by the yardstick of Gloucester's corresponding economic decline. But success came at a heavy price. Just as the shift from fishing to granite to art colony required adjustment, the boom in tourism was not without a detrimental effect on the workings and soul of the art colony. Granted, tourism was important, especially for the artists who thrived on a continual market for their artwork, but there could also be too much of a good thing.

The change was a gradual one, spread over the late '50s and early '60s. For starters, the requisite cheap space for artists was no longer available, as the "discovery" of the town inevitably caused property values to rise. Many young artists who required affordable homes with studio space, not to mention gallery or exhibit space, were priced out of Rockport. There were also basic logistical issues: there was no longer room on the crowded wharves to accommodate forty or more painters. And what some have declared a defining criterion of an art colony—namely, a place where painters can work without being disturbed—was also no longer being met. The sheer volume of tourists, along with a lack of respect for the privacy of an artist at work, made it increasingly difficult to paint outside. The halcyon days of the large *plein air* classes were over.

Larger, more core issues were also precipitating change. Mirroring societal changes throughout America, Rockport could not help but lose some of its small-town innocence. The evolution of American art after the end of World War II, with modernism coming to the forefront, also made a qualitative difference. Suddenly, the realists in Rockport were swimming against the artistic current and, even if they prospered locally, were likely to get snubbed by the major "leading edge" galleries in New York and elsewhere. While the Rockport Art Association continued to anchor the art community, individual artists were going more their own ways, and the cohesiveness of the artistic community had lost some of its glue, perhaps partly because Hibbard was no longer at the helm. Nonetheless, young artists who had arrived immediately after World War II would continue the art colony tradition, as would subsequent generations of painters who would settle in Rockport over the ensuing years, open galleries of their own and perpetuate the realistic Rockport style. (Plates 25–27)

The ability to "take it" is built deep into a Ford

RIGHT FROM THE START, the Ford car has won a good reputation for its ability to go and keep going with minimum trouble or expense.

Today there are nearly 7 million Ford cars in service in America, of which close to 2 million are over 10 years old and still going strong, with another 2 million now 5 to 10 years old.

Partly, that record has been established as the result of the great number of Ford cars that have been built. But partly, also, it is a direct result of the *way* they have been built.

In its design, materials, and workmanship, the quality of a Ford car is calculated not only to please you as you buy, but to serve and serve you well far beyond the first year or two or three that you may drive it.

Naturally, we do not ask you today to buy a Ford just because it will last a long time. We invite you to compare our present car on the basis of whatever points you yourself set greatest store by in selecting an automobile.

Choose for power, choose for style, choose for roominess, choose for riding ease. If you make your choice with care, you are pretty apt to wind up with a 1941 Ford. And when you do, you may feel sure that beneath the things you chose it for is that other thing that every Ford has had — the car is built to "take it" for a long, long time. If you own a Ford, time will prove the wisdom of your choice!

Some Ford Advantages for 1941:

NEW ROOMINESS. Bodies are longer and wider this year, adding as much as seven inches to seating width.

SOFT, QUIET RIDE. A new Ford ride, with new frame and stabilizer, softer springs, improved shock absorbers.

POWER WITH ECONOMY. This year, more than ever, Ford owners are enthusiastic about the economy and fine all-round performance of Ford cars.

BIG WINDOWS. Windshield and windows increased all around to give nearly four square feet of added vision area in each '41 Ford Sedan.

LARGEST HYDRAULIC BRAKES in the Ford price field give added safety, longer brake-lining wear.

Ford

GET THE FACTS...
AND YOU'LL GET A **FORD**

This advertisement will appear in *Life*, July 21; *Saturday Evening Post*, July 26; *U. S. Coast Guard Magazine* (B&W), August and *U. S. News* (B&W), July 11.

FWO 5078; P. O. 8283 AD FC/91

IMAGE 23. Ford advertisement, "The ability to 'take it' is built deep into a Ford," 1941 [14 x 10½ in.] The Motif is buoy-less, as would be anticipated; what is inexplicable is why the female artist in the foreground has her back turned to the two most paintable subjects within eye-range: Motif No. 1 and the shiny new Ford. *From the Collections of Henry Ford.*

Image 24. Kodak advertisement, "Don't 'spend' your vacation—save it, with snapshots," 1952 [14 x 10 $^3/_8$ in.]. The Motif as a spokes-shack for Kodak film is a perfect fit. Note the large number of buoys now hanging on the side of the shack. *Collection of the author.*

The Motif itself underwent major changes as well. A record-setting year for northeasters in the winter of 1957–58 undermined the shack's foundation, resulting in an alarming sag in its southeast corner. The reconstruction plan included pouring concrete around the foundation and also straightening the shack. Hibbard, still on the Motif No. 1 Committee, reluctantly agreed to the concrete but was adamantly opposed to correcting the list, exclaiming, "You wouldn't straighten up the Leaning Tower of Pisa!" In this, of course, Hibbard would be proven incorrect, since the latter structure ultimately required structural straightening, as did Motif No. 1, under the direction of, appropriately enough, an Italian contractor named Salvatore Bianchini.[192]

While Bianchini was doing his best to straighten the Motif and still preserve its showy decrepitude, the shack was gaining more exposure on the international stage. The Motif had already increased its national exposure by moonlighting as a model for Madison Avenue as early as 1940. (Plate 28) Then came a prominent cameo role in television with the 1957 premiere of *The Harbormaster* on CBS. Starring Barry Sullivan, this series ran for twenty-five episodes (ABC picked up the second season, renaming it *Adventure at Scott Island*) and was set on a fictional island near Rockport. Filming crews at Rockport Harbor and Bearskin Neck, of course, contributed to the already chaotic tourist season.

But the largest stage of all was the 1958 World's Fair in Brussels, where a Circle-Vision Disneyland film called *America the Beautiful* made its debut. This movie-in-the-round presentation created by means of multiple projector technology featured a water-level approach into Rockport Harbor that lasted for thirty seconds, with nearly seven of those seconds spent panning past the Motif. During this segment, the omniscient narrator posed the question: "Where did this drive for the American dream begin?" and answered himself: "Not just in the great cities, but in towns and hamlets all over colonial America. The spirit of the early settlers is still all around us, hundreds of years later."[193]

The film opened in the Circarama Theater in Disneyland's Tomorrowland in June 1960 and ran until September 1966, after which a reshot version debuted the following year. Two subsequent revised versions of the film were shown until the beginning of 1984.[194] Even fine art can't hold a candle to the Magic Kingdom, if one town leader's comments to the *New York Times* mean anything: "'It's a symbol of the town and it's a symbol of New England,' explained Frederick Tarr 3d, one of the town selectmen...'Heck, it's a national symbol—if you go to Disneyland one of the first things you see is a movie that includes a ride into Rockport Harbor and a view of the motif.'"[195]

More publicity brought more visitors and more recognition for Rockport beyond anything the Board of Trade could accomplish by itself. Rockport had long since decimated Gloucester in the tourist wars, and to the victor went the spoils, such as they were. Hibbard had seen the changes coming and already sounded wistful in 1939. Interviewed again in 1964, Hibbard readily admitted that two-thirds of the material to paint in Rockport was gone and that the town had lost 50 percent of its charm.[196] But if he couldn't bring back the cows near his house or the schooners or the fishermen repairing and tarring their nets on the wharf, he at least still had some say about Motif No. 1.

Back at the shack, Bill Donovan, Yuk Mackay and the rest of the lobsterman gang continued to build and repair the lobster traps and fashion and paint the buoys. The cast of characters would change over the years, but among themselves, the men shared four stalls downstairs. Steve Orr and George Soine were both in the shack until about 1962. A lobsterman named Walter "Onion" Rich used a stall until about 1958. Edward "Slippery" Wiitanen took out fishing parties and mainly used his space for storage. The occupancy of the shack was a good deal, with informal arrangements with the town and no specific leases or fees for storage of lobster pots on the wharf. Of course, there were no toilet facilities, no electricity and not even a lock on the door. And while going about their business, the lobstermen chose not to dwell on the fact that they served an additional role, one they neither sought, wanted nor were paid for: providing local color for the tourists.

DISASTER!

When Don Atkinson was hired as Rockport's director of public works in 1972, Selectman Nick Barletta drove him around town, pointing out all the buildings that would be under his purview. An old fish house on the end of a wharf was not "just another building," Atkinson realized, when Barletta emphasized its history and informed the new hire that "it's your responsibility and you better make sure that it stays the same. Nobody wants any change."

So it was a rough seventy-two hours for Atkinson and the rest of the townspeople when the two-day Blizzard of '78 began on Monday, February 6. The devastating storm caused nearly $1.4 million in property damage on Bearskin Neck alone; nearly two hundred houses and cottages were damaged and nine totally destroyed, nine boats were damaged or sunk, commercial firms sustained over $200,000 in losses and costs to repair public and private retaining walls, breakwaters and piers were estimated at $7 million.[197] And if that weren't bad enough, Motif No. 1, Rockport's "sacred monument," was completely decimated.

IMAGE 25. This photograph of Motif No. 1, shot at 9:00 a.m. on February 6, 1978, is very possibly the last photograph ever taken of the intact original fish house. *Collection of Buddy Woods.*

IMAGE 26. After the blizzard. The single-story section of the Motif is collapsed upon the wharf. The two-story section, which was lying atop the *Calypso* in the aftermath of the storm, fell into the north basin of the harbor once the dragger was moved away and had already been removed from the water prior to the taking of this photo. *Courtesy of the Sandy Bay Historical Society.*

Buddy Woods, a former department of public works commissioner and Rockport selectman (and grandson of Dana Vibert), was on the fire department at the time. When he came out of the Masonic Lodge at about 9:30 p.m. that Monday evening, snow was blowing horizontally up Broadway. That night, he and other members of the fire and police departments were called out to assist in evacuations, while the Red Cross set up a shelter at the high school. By the following morning, eighteen to twenty inches of snow had fallen, winds up to sixty-five miles per hour had been reported, whitecaps were in the streets and floodwaters were threatening homes. Bearskin Neck was completely evacuated, with electricity preventively cut off in the overhead lines in Dock Square by the Massachusetts Electric Company, given the fear of explosion from broken gas lines. A spokesperson for the utility company reported: "Rockport is really getting sacked."[198]

When Atkinson—who also assumed the roles of civil defense director and disaster coordinator—and Barletta and Harbormaster Gene "Shorty" Lesch were assessing damage to Bearskin Neck on the morning of February 7, water was covering the wharves and parked cars were floating; at least five washed into the harbor. The high tide mark of about fourteen feet had remained essentially unchanged during low tide, so they were worried. As the three men stood at the near end of T-Wharf, watching the anchored boats in the harbor rise to the level of the wharves themselves, they were particularly concerned about Walt Whitaker's thirty-five-foot dragger *Calypso*, which was tied to the Motif's wharf and threatening to rise onto the wharf itself. Structural damage to the wharf was likely if that occurred, but the men could only watch helplessly. Lesch and Atkinson had always worked well together and been clear about their respective responsibilities: "It's *my* water, it's *your* wharf," Harbormaster Lesch would say to Public Works Director Atkinson. As the *Calypso* bobbed and roiled in the waves and water covered the wharf, the previously clear-cut job descriptions had descended into an unfortunate ambiguity.

And then the three men saw a huge wall of water coming over the breakwater, what they would later realize was a "rogue wave," which Atkinson estimated as being ten to fifteen feet higher than Bearskin Neck (the *New York Times* reported that "walls of water 30 to 40 feet high" smashed into the picturesque seacoast).[199]

Barletta was quoted: "I told [Atkinson] that I thought I saw the old Motif move, then we ducked for cover for five minutes."[200]

Neither Barletta, Atkinson nor Lesch witnessed the wave lifting the shack up from its foundation and crashing it back down on the granite. The next time they looked, Motif No. 1 had collapsed and was leaning against the *Calypso*.

News of the collapse was broadcast on national network newscasts and as far away as West Germany.[201] The *Gloucester Daily Times* reported that during the height of the storm, scores of people had stood on Main Street, Atlantic Avenue and by the entrance to T-Wharf to look at the shattered remains of their beloved shack. Selectmen Barletta and Ted Tarr were unable to comment on the value of the town's loss. They echoed exactly the same sentiments regarding the Motif's value: it was inestimable.[202] And neither was referring to the value of the shack to the town's coffers but to the value of Motif No. 1 in the town's heart.

MOTIF AS PHOENIX

A week after the storm, the Public Works Department began dismantling the Motif's remains, removing the boards piece by piece and saving "everything red" in a storage area in the town's sewage treatment buildings.[203] Before

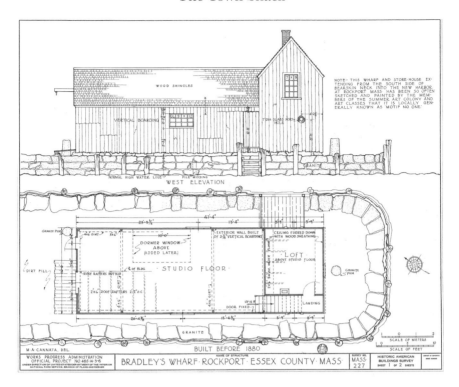

IMAGE 27. *Bradley's Wharf, Bearskin Neck, Rockport, Essex, MA,* Sheet 1 of 2 [18 x 24 in.]. *Library of Congress, Prints and Photographs Division, Historic American Buildings Survey, Reproduction Number HABS MASS, 5-ROCPO, 1-. www.loc.gov/pictures/item/ma0676.*

that, on Wednesday, February 8, the *Gloucester Daily Times* was already reporting that the Motif would be rebuilt, possibly with federal dollars. The cost of rebuilding the shack was estimated at $15,000, with local carpenters immediately offering their services gratis. Fortunately, back in 1965, former director of the Department of Public Works Salty Owen had sent Police Chief Louis Anderson to photograph the Motif and have town employees take exact measurements of the building, in case it were destroyed by fire.[204] Owens needn't have bothered, had he known or remembered that the Motif had been measured and drawn by the Historic American Buildings Survey in the spring of 1938.

A committee of residents was formed to oversee fundraising and rebuilding and consisted of the existing Motif No. 1 Committee (Homer Orne, Dana Vibert and Buddy Woods) and two representatives each from the Board of Trade, the Bearskin Neck Association, the Rockport Art Association and the Rotary Club, plus a representative of the fishermen (Jack Burbank). The town had no insurance coverage for the Motif, and the committee decided against applying for FEMA funds, opting for private funding by the people of Rockport.

Aside from a general reluctance to relinquish control of the project to the government, the committee was sensitive to the plight of storm victims and did not want to compete for federal dollars when other Rockporters had more pressing needs: the loss of homes, businesses or boats. Also, they recognized that the choice to rebuild was not universally favored. Dr. William Hoyt, at the time the president of the Sandy Bay Historical Society, was outspoken in his opposition to the project, feeling that the shack should be left to memory. While he generally was a proponent of restoration, rebuilding was another thing altogether; he saw no reason for "erecting a false shack now that an act of God has taken the original away." Clearly, his overriding philosophy may have been colored by a widely held ambivalence toward tourism, an appreciation of the incoming business but resentful of the intrusions. Quoting Hoyt: "The merchants like it [the Motif] because it helps their business. But if the Motif is rebuilt to attract more people—well, I don't think we need more people."[205] But Hoyt was in the minority, and his viewpoint did not take into account the basic truth at the heart of it all: most Rockporters did not want to lose the landscape of their youth.

The expanded Motif No. 1 Committee wasted no time in distributing canisters around town for collecting funds, along with posters provided by the Rockport Art Association. A photograph book was printed and sold for fundraising. While initially it had been hoped that the original floor planks, doors and window frames could be incorporated into the new building, an assessment of the remains of the shack deemed this unfeasible. No original timber would be used in the new building, and timber fragments would be mementos only; specifically, they would not be sold to finance rebuilding, as suggested by Jack Burbank. Burbank's proposal was rejected as being too commercial; the idea of selling relics of a treasured town symbol to tourists even now seems downright sacrilegious. The only tangible material that would be shared by both the original and new Motif would be the bronze dedication plaque from 1950.

Ultimately, more than $20,000 was raised by individual contributors by the end of July. As early as March, the committee was confident that it would not need to rely on volunteers and began reviewing estimates from contractors. Workers began restoration on July 28, and on the morning of August 2, the new concrete foundation was poured in preparation for the new post and beam structure. For the siding and roof, contractor George Hobbs

132

had outbid the competition by a paltry $250, likely garnering $10,000 in free advertising, he laughingly admits (Hobbs has had a Motif logo on every truck he's owned since that time). Mindful of the townspeople's desire to "rebuild it like it was," Hobbs offered to replicate the previous swale in the shack's roof, but the committee rejected the idea, considering it impossible to attempt to truly duplicate the original building. On October 21, 1978, members of the Rotary Club arrived at 8:00 a.m. to paint the new Motif using brushes furnished by the local hardware store, J. Raymond Smith, and paint, donated by the Cabot Company, from the Gloucester Building Center. Finally, on Sunday, November 26, the ribbon-cutting ceremony was held. "The new Motif was formally accepted by the town and opened for use by local fishermen in a brief ceremony yesterday at Bradley Wharf. About 20 people gathered in the cold, crisp weather to watch Selectman chairman Nicola Barletta cut the ribbon on the new building."[206]

The event proceeded without fanfare: no bands, no Legionnaires, no swarms of press and photographers, no reenactments, no crowds. The Board of Trade had no need to make a play for more tourism. Few serious artists were painting the shack to any great extent at this point, and with reluctance or mixed feelings when doing so. Hardly any of the key players of the original Rockport Art Colony were alive to witness the demise of the shack that had been so important to them and to which they in turn had been so instrumental. Aldro Hibbard had died in 1972, Thieme in 1954, Hornby in 1956, Buckley in 1958 and Cady in 1970. Emile Gruppé, who once had the temerity to ask "What if something should happen to Jack Buckley's shack and there wasn't any Motif No. 1 anymore?" was alive when the Motif went down but did not live to see the completion of its replacement, dying on September 28, 1978.

For Buddy Woods and the rest of the committee, the project was done, and they were ready to move forward. The ribbon cutting was simply that; there were new tenants with signed leases waiting to move in and use the shack for storage. Rockport had a Motif No. 1 again, and the time would soon come when most tourists coming to town would not know, or care, that there had ever been another.

Chapter 10

The View from the Wharf

In Which the Narrator Recognizes that He Is No Longer Your Average Tourist

On a beautiful Sunday in August, Rockport is teeming with tourists. Once again I am standing on the end of T-Wharf—as I have become in the habit of doing—looking at Motif No. 1. No longer confused, I am only contemplative. Earlier in the day, I had browsed through the final summer exhibit at the Rockport Art Association. Ninety-six works of art were on display, and I was not at all surprised to find that not a single one contained a depiction of the Motif.

Today, a luxury boat is tied to the wharf and a couple of families are aboard, kids romping along the deck, the men shirtless, sitting in deck chairs drinking Budweiser. I am pondering the etherealness of the picturesque when a middle-aged husband and wife—whom I later learn are visiting from the south shore of New Jersey—approach me tentatively.

"Is this...is this the famous fish shack...?" the woman asks me, pointing weakly.

"Yes," I reply authoritatively, "Motif No. 1."

"I thought so," she says. "My friend told me it was red."

In Which the Narrator Penetrates the Façade

Arnold Knauth, who is ninety-three and still painting, first came to Rockport in 1939 to study with Aldro Hibbard. He spent three summers in Rockport before being drafted; after the war, he relocated there permanently. From his house on Atlantic Avenue, he has looked across the harbor at the Motif every day for nearly sixty-five years. Before I visited him recently, Arnold had rummaged around his home/studio and dug up a Motif painting to show me. In a houseful of paintings, this was the only representation of the Motif that he had left; all the others had been sold.

I asked Arnold if the painting predated the Blizzard of '78, but he wasn't sure. We both turned our attention to his painting for a few moments of examination. The original Motif, I knew, had a swale in the roof and the wharf pilings were of different heights, but Arnold was a painter, not a photographer. Finally, he shrugged. "I can't tell, can you?"

And what did it matter, anyway?

Arnold then told me that in the winter of 1978 he had felt an urge to see the inside of the Motif, something he had never done, despite having painted it too many times to remember. Up to that point, only the outside had ever held any interest for him. While his paintings conveyed the narrative that fishing activities took place inside, the actual inside was invisible and irrelevant, as was the norm. Still, for no apparent reason, Arnold suddenly wanted to see what was there. He considered it a premonition of sorts, since within the month, the old fish shack would be gone.

"So what did you see? I mean, when you went inside?" I asked him. I already knew the answer and couldn't even hold back a smile.

"Nothing much," he said, smiling back. "Just an old shack with stuff hanging in it."

Arnold's description holds true for the most part, except now the inside belongs to a relatively new shack. Within its walls, the Motif can have no pretensions to age: despite the old time post and beam construction, the corners are square, the wood is dimensional; the materials—from the nails to the plywood sheathing—are conventional and modern. The downstairs is a nondescript storage space with six stalls that are leased out for between $250 and $500 a year, depending on their size (roughly ninety cents a square foot). The harbormaster has use of one of the stalls, and five others store a variety of fishing paraphernalia. Bill Donovan and Yuk Mackey were the last lobstermen to actually use the inside as a workspace, and even they had no more real work to do after 1974. From a working shack standpoint, Motif No. 1 had gone into retirement once wooden lobster traps and buoys became obsolete.

The upstairs is another story. Originally, this was the office for the fish broker; Buckley had fixed it up so his friend Jerry Fitzpatrick would have a place to stay; in the '50s and '60s there had been a small table and an automobile seat facing the window, where the lobsterman in free moments could relax and enjoy the view out to sea. Jack Burbank took possession of the space in 1968 and was most responsible for the preservation of the remaining artifacts. Currently, Captain Bill Lee, the last trawler captain operating out of Rockport, holds the lease for the second story. Having been one of the initial renters of a downstairs stall, he moved upstairs when Burbank retired and inherited nearly all the diverse objects that Burbank had collected, some of them salvaged after the blizzard and dating back from Buckley's time in the shack and earlier. A few of the artifacts were donated to the Thatcher Island Museum, but nearly every square inch of wall space, table space and no small portion of floor space is covered with old photographs, signs, fishing implements and other unanticipated memorabilia. The collection continues to expand, as over the years, Lee and other Rockport locals regularly convene in the shack to hang out and reminisce. Objects are brought and left, seemingly at random.

"Where did *that* come from?" I asked Captain Lee, pointing at something that caught my eye.

IMAGE 28. Southeast corner of second-story space of Motif No. 1, occupied by Captain Bill Lee. © *copyright 2011 Robert M. Ring.*

"Can't really remember," he answered. "Been hanging there twenty or thirty years at least. Somebody must have brought it."

I had the sense that a new history was being written and each object was an undocumented clue, its meaning already lost to memory.

More than fascinated, I was transfixed and unexpectedly moved. The space was a sanctuary, humble yet hallowed. Even the small electric light on the sill of the second-story window, kept lit by Captain Lee out of respect for our war veterans (Lee himself is ex-navy and served in Vietnam), packed the spiritual punch of an expanse of votive candles. Nowhere had I encountered the true spirit of the Motif so preserved, the shack so honored and respected, traditions perpetuated, than in Captain Lee's second-story space.

Outside attentions, to be truthful, were fickle and perhaps folly. But inside, here was the true Motive, comfortable in its own skin.

IN WHICH THE NARRATOR ACCOUNTS FOR A SHED'S FAME AND GLORY

The couple from New Jersey had discovered Motif No. 1, and I watched as they took pictures of it. Thinking back to the beginning of my journey, I could relate. They knew it had been painted a lot, they knew it was something they needed to see when visiting Rockport, Massachusetts. I'm not sure what else they made of it, other than the usual, of course. It and the town were quaint and picturesque, albeit crowded. And they must have figured that the shack was certainly old. In my own convoluted way, I had also found the Motif after a fashion—search completed, questions answered, curiosity satisfied about how and why this particular fish shack had come to be what it was.

Artists and tourists had to be given their due, but they were aided by a fortuitous historic circumstance: Motif No. 1 came of age during a convergence of a period of "national" tourism and an American scene/ regionalist movement in art. Unlike the mass tourism that developed after the Second World War, tourists from 1880 until about 1940 were looking for an authentic America and turning to the past to discover a shared national history and culture.[207] The myth of an "Old New England" reflected this colonial past, and it did not matter that the fish shack was a late nineteenth-century structure—the Motif masqueraded as part of the tradition simply through its existence in a town with a colonial and fishing past and a proud Yankee heritage. Within the encompassing time frame of national tourism, American artists during the interwar period had come to recognize that they no longer needed to rely on Europe for artistic standards or aesthetic guidance. Partly as a counter to modernism, and later as a response to the Depression, groups of American artists discovered America's own "useable past" and made it the subject of their paintings. These paintings were "of a place" and as much about local culture as geography.

The margins of artistic "mini-movements" are difficult to define, but the Rockport artists, generally realistic or naturalistic painters, blended the picturesque with the regional to portray idealized scenes of a New England coastal community that were accessible and appealing to a general audience. And while Hibbard and other members of the colony took on certain stylistic qualities that have led to the designation of a "Rockport School"—which art historian Richard H. Love describes as assimilation of "a technique that included a mid-range palette (frequently including black), broadly brushed forms, a strong expressionistic treatment of water reflections, and a penchant to depict the effect of Cape Ann's special light"—a wide range of styles has always been in evidence. The notion of an all-encompassing Rockport School is a myth. What really linked the artists were the picturesque subject matter and a decision to paint in Rockport, which was "virtually a kaleidoscope collection of picturesque American scenes, a sparking treasure chest on earth for any realist painter."[208] The motif of the Motif, so to speak—the composition of the wharf, shack and boats—was only one of many picturesque scenes near at hand. But it was…well, right *there*.

There was much more to it, as we have seen. The colony of artists had the energetic Aldro Hibbard as their leader and, largely through the force of his personality and efforts, acquired the reputation of collegiality and social cohesiveness that attracted both artists and art enthusiasts. Hibbard and his colleagues did all they could to promote their work and their community by establishing a distinctive brand—exploiting the Motif quite effectively to these ends—that expressed a conviction that the art coming out of Rockport was somehow different from that being produced elsewhere on Cape Ann. The distinction was an artificial one. Whether through Aldro Hibbard's and the American Legion's civic bolstering, or the community of painters and sculptors and the art they produced, or Dixie Johnston's antics, or the Rockport Art Association and the events and exhibitions they sponsored, or the Board of Trade and their promotional campaigns, Motif No. 1 did not become a cultural icon because it was inevitable. The motivation for all these actions was rooted primarily in individual or collective economic necessity, and the actions themselves were conscious, premeditated and often shamelessly self-promoting.

And they were successful. The Motif stands as a tangible testament to the success of those efforts, which themselves have otherwise largely been forgotten. The quote below, which is in specific reference to tourism, could not more aptly apply to the rise and transformation of Motif No. 1:

> *Tourism is not destiny, imposed on a community or a region by its geography or its history. Tourist industries were built by people. Sometimes they were created by individual entrepreneurs...sometimes Corporations...state governments...even families...But in every case, the industries were the products of human choices, made not only by visitors, but by natives as well. Those choices were often made under extreme economic duress; they were often made by outside investors "for" the inhabitants of a place, or by a small minority of more powerful inhabitants against the will of others. Certainly they were influenced and shaped by economic and even geographic forces larger than the community themselves. But they were not predetermined.*[209]

Along the way, the Motif became so ingrained in the collective consciousness of the town that its duplicate had to be built in the exact spot of its shattered remains. Not for the artists or for the tourists, but for the people of Rockport themselves. In a community that had continually been forced to reinvent itself, the fish shack had come to represent a constancy, an unbreakable link to the past and a reminder that not everything had to change in Rockport. There it still stands, and there is no small measure of comfort in that.

In Which the Narrator Ponders a Plethora of Narratives

Another reason for the fish shack's success was that it lent itself easily to an idealized and sought-after narrative. An ad for the Thieme Gallery that appeared on the back cover of the 1952 *Rockport Anchor* sums up the narrative quite well: "In old Rockport for many years Anthony Thieme has been painting its old wharves, charming crooked streets, Cape Ann houses aged and gentle, incorporating into his canvasses the passing life of the people who have made this New England village a place to be remembered."

The shack's presence in the landscape revealed the culture of the town and conveyed the story of what the people did and how they lived. As a still life, the fish shack epitomized the seafaring culture of old New England. There was never any sense of interior or need of one; the exterior was emblematic of an oceanic environment and clearly gave a sense of the days spent by the local people. This is the narrative of Motif No. 1 or, more accurately, the original one.

More recently, this traditional narrative accounts for the Motif's forays into Hollywood, where it has been repeatedly cast as a scene-setting backdrop. In the 1998 film *The Love Letter*, the Motif is a fish shack in a fictional town of Loblolly by the Sea. In *Stuck on You* (2003), the Motif portrays a fish shack in Nantucket. Most recently, in the 2009 film *The Proposal*, the fish shack demonstrates its versatility as a thespian by seamlessly assuming the role of a fish shack in Sitka, Alaska. So much for the New England narrative, one might think. But all it took to modify the narrative was the superimposition of another image that would immediately express a different culture: in this case, a piece of Inuit art hanging alongside the buoys (and for the dullards in the audience, a sign that spelled out "Sitka, Alaska.") Voilà, the Yankee maritime tradition is supplanted by an Aleutian one.

Significantly, the original narrative for the fish house has been modified or transformed over the course of its history, either by the superimposition of new narratives upon the old one or the supplanting of the old narrative altogether. Consider the watercolor by the Gloucester artist Joseph Margulies, executed sometime in the '30s. (Plate 23) Rather than depicting a fish house as representative of a fishing culture, the narrative is that of a fish house as an artistic subject. Beneath that particular narrative, of course, is the unstated assumption that there is a good reason for this shack to be painted, including: the scene is picturesque, the scene is uncomplicated enough for amateur artists to tackle and, for those in the know, because the Motif is famous and everyone has to paint it at least once. Regardless of how we "read" the picture, the narrative is obviously not the same one as most of the other examples already presented here. For a movie equivalent of this narrative, albeit subtle enough to be classified as an "inside joke," astute observers have noted the painting of Motif No. 1 hanging on the wall of the dentist's office in *Finding Nemo* (2003), the animated film written and directed by Rockport native Andrew Staunton (who also includes a picture of the Twin Lighthouses at Thatcher's Island).

Then we come to an oil painting by the late William Bradley that itself has become iconic as a popular print, postcard and, most notably, poster. (Plate 29) Entitled *Icon 1*, the piece is brilliant partly because of its unmistakably wry narrative. This is not about a shack representing a fishing culture or about a maritime artistic subject but rather about a shack that is iconic. In this admittedly tongue-in-cheek representation, Motif No. 1, adorned with 24K gold leaf and Eastern Orthodox Christian symbols, is both literally and figuratively an icon.

I refer to this particular Motif-related state of affairs as "narrative confusion." Not only did it cause my befuddlement upon first encountering the Motif, but I suspect that one reason the Motif is so infrequently tackled by painters these days is because it is overladen with its various narratives. Karen Quinn, curator of paintings, Art of the Americas at the Museum of Fine Arts in Boston, admitted that with Motif paintings, "the hard part is seeing past the layers of meaning." Narrative confusion is different and more nuanced than plain overexposure, to which the Motif is also an undeniable victim. Serious painters are not drawn to subjects displayed on trinkets and souvenirs, as if the value of their work might be diminished by subject association. Representations of the Motif are well suited to all varieties of folksy arts and crafts or gift items, such as place mats, drink coasters and

IMAGE 29. Motif No. 1 place mat by Sarah Elizabeth Holloran (1917–2009), 1977. Wood block print on cotton [13¼ x 18¾ in.]. Holloran was a member of the Folly Cove Designers for twenty-seven years; this depiction of the Motif was the last full-sized wood block she produced. *Courtesy of Isabel Natti, the Sarah Elizabeth Shop, Rockport, Massachusetts (photographic reproduction by Linda A. Marquette).*

cartoon satires, since not only can these objects be created without artistic angst but they share a clear, common narrative: of a red fish shack that symbolizes the town of Rockport, Massachusetts (with the implicit corollary: "I've been there and brought this back"). Other narratives, for all intents and purposes, do not come into play.

Painters in Rockport are cognizant of the historical importance of the fish house and feel a responsibility to protect the reputation of Rockport as a town that produces fine paintings. As artists, they do not want their work to be derivative; they want neither to be restricted thematically nor to sacrifice artistic integrity. If they eschew portraying the Motif, it is not through any sense of intimidation but by choice. A well-known Rockport artist told me that one could paint the Motif as long as it was done in a unique and different way. This, of course, is a challenge that dates as far back as the 1930s, when, as we have seen, painters sought a variety of angles: front side, back side, side side, from the wharf, from the shore, from across the harbor, from in the harbor, from above—with all the combinations and permutations of adjacent boats, weather and lighting conditions. One approach is to downplay the shack, relegating it to a non-starring role in a general harbor scene, as it was often painted in its pre-fame days. (Plates 8 and 9)

Another artist I spoke with admitted that the Motif remains a subject that can be made into a beautiful painting, and as such, "I have interest in it on occasion." At the same time, he admitted that he would be in for a ribbing if caught in the act of painting it, with artist buddies likely to quip something along the lines of "Painting a Thieme?" or "Painting for the tourists, are you?" He admitted that as a younger painter, he was more likely to make the mistake of painting the shack as a "portrait" rather than a "stage," not fully understanding that "the composition and color were free, it was up to me." The most successful paintings, now, as in the past, are of a scene—not a shack—that is evocative and atmospheric. I include examples from three contemporary Rockport painters: Donald Mosher, Tom Nicholas and David Tutwiler. (Plates 30–32) These depictions of the Motif all convey a sense of a New England coastal town and fishing community but with a contemporary narrative. In these stories told through paint on canvas, the Motif is neither a relic of the past, nor a self-conscious model, nor the face of a town; still, it is capable of inspiring.

In Which the Narrator Surveys His Scene from the Wharf

The couple from New Jersey has left to wander around town; perhaps they are buying fudge in the retail space where Albert Story, and then Sweeney Hanson, once sold fish. So for the moment I have the wharf all to myself. I am looking long and hard at a red fish shack.

I silently apologize to Motif No. 1 for all the times I have considered it, or referred to it, as a cliché. Certainly many paintings of it are clichés, and its commercial exploitation often makes it seem like a cliché. Yet it has no pretenses of being anything other than what it is: a simple fish house on the end of an old granite wharf that has consistently remained unassuming as a variety of roles have been placed upon it. Passively and patiently, it has stood there as people have fussed over it, written about it, painted and photographed it, as bands have played for it and choruses sung to it, as people have made money off it. It has been accessorized not only with buoys but also with flags, pennants, wreaths, bows and Inuit art. Such is the price of celebrity, and the Motif never asked for any of it. After all, this is just a fish shack.

Aldro Hibbard was right when he admitted in the euphoria of the parade float success in 1933 that the fish house itself is not interesting and would be commonplace were it not for the boats that come against it. There are no schooners at its side today—there rarely are anymore—so Motif No. 1 is undoubtedly even more commonplace now than it was in the past. The lobster boats in the harbor are compositionally too small in scale, with too low a profile. They could do well with larges masts and sails, I think—those strong vertical elements are lacking in photographs these days, as in the scene before my eyes. And on this hot August day, a luxury cruiser tied alongside with shirtless men drinking beer is not exactly an element I would choose to include in my composition. But it occurs to me—and I can't believe it never did before—that the Motif in reality is not, and never has been, as picturesque, atmospheric or evocative as in its portrayals. Artists worth their salt don't simply paint what they see but what they feel, and Motif No. 1 truthfully doesn't do its own paintings justice. Only the paintings—not the real thing—can take my breath away.

Still, the legacy of Motif No. 1 is more than its ability to inspire artists but perhaps the ability to inspire the artist in all of us. Before me is a scene, a living still life that I can compose without paints or canvas. I can stand where I am or walk around and consider my still life from any variety of angles. I can move to Bradley Wharf or see how things look from Atlantic Avenue. Maybe I will catch a quick glimpse from my car window as I drive by or as I walk past an alleyway or look from my table in a restaurant, framing my composition by windowpanes. I can wait for the weather to change, wait for the right cloud pattern, wait for the fog to come in or go out. And if conditions aren't quite right (and even Thieme would cover a dozen canvases before coming up with a really good one), I can return some other time. I can compose my still life in any season, in the snow or rain, at daybreak, twilight or evening, when a small light shines from the second-story window.

Best of all, I am an invisible part of the still life in my field of vision. Not merely looking; I am encompassed by these surroundings, a participant in my own maritime tableaux. And as I compose and process my scene, I can smell the salt air and feel the heat of the sun on my skin.

A breeze musses my hair.

I reach for my camera.

Notes

CHAPTER 1

1. Don Guy, "Rockport Does One-Side Job on 'Motif.' Most Famous Shack Gets Coat of Paint," *Boston Daily Globe*, May 18, 1959.
2. Richard Fay Warner, "Rockport—Home of Motif Number One," *New York Times*, June 24, 1951.
3. Meyer Berger, "Rugged Rockport. The Town Where the Glacier Stopped Is a Briny Paradise for Artists," *New York Times*, August 31, 1947.
4. "Motif Is No. 1 on Travel Brochures," *Gloucester Daily Times*, March 19, 1988; "Rockport Ramblings. Motif No. 1 Receives Outrageous Exposure," *Gloucester Daily Times*, February 20, 1988.
5. "Maine-iacs Filch Our Motif! Their Faces Lobster-Red," *Gloucester Daily Times*, November 27, 1962.
6. Herbert Kenney, "Every Crime Has a Motif: Rockport's Arty Symbol Stolen Again," *Boston Globe*, November 27, 1962.
7. Personal communications, December 23 and 24, 2006.
8. John L. Cooley, *Rockport Sketch Book* (Rockport, MA: Rockport Art Association, 1965).
9. Leslie D. Bartlett, "Motif No.1—The Little Fish Shack Which Refused to Go Away,™" *Gloucester Daily Times*, April 4, 2002, and www.rockportusa.com/motifone/column040402.html.

CHAPTER 2

10. Registry of Deeds, Southern Essex District, Salem, Massachusetts, Book 294, 197–99.

11. Log of the Minutes of the Sandy Bay Pier Company, in the collection of the Sandy Bay Historical Society.

12. From the transcription of the Journals of Ebenezer Pool at the Sandy Bay Historical Society, Vol. 2, 44.

13. George Brown Goode, *The Fisheries and Fishing Industries of the United States, Section II* (Washington, D.C.: Government Printing Office, 1887), 144.

14. John W. Marshall, Henry Dennis, Newell Burnham and Levi Cleaves, eds., *History of the Town of Rockport, as Comprised in the Centennial Address of Lemuel Gott, M.D., Extracts from the Memoranda of Ebenezer Pool, Esq., and Interesting Items from Other Sources* (Rockport, MA: Rockport Review Office, 1888), 41, 80, 288; Captain Sylvanus Smith, *Fisheries of Cape Ann: A Collection of Reminiscent Narratives of Fishing and Coasting Trips; Descriptive Stories of "Sandy Bay" and "The Harbor"; Also Some Interesting Comment on Fisheries Legislation and Cause of the Decline of the Fisheries; with a Prophetic Glimpse into the Future* (Gloucester, MA: Press of Gloucester Times Co., 1915), 11, 112.

15. Samuel Eliot Morison, *The Maritime History of Massachusetts, 1783–1860* (Boston: Northeastern University Press, 1979), 302.

16. Smith, *Fisheries of Cape Ann*, 102.

17. Goode, *Fisheries and Fishing Industries of the United States*, 141.

18. Ibid., 149.

19. Ibid., 142.

20. From the transcribed summary of the minutes of the Sandy Bay Pier Company, in the collection of the Sandy Bay Historical Society, compiled by Eleanor Parson, 1998, 17–18.

21. Eleanor Parsons compiled transcripts, 25.

22. Marshall et al., *History of the Town of Rockport*, 229.

23. Harbor of Refuge Committee, *Harbor of Refuge at Sandy Bay, Cape Ann, Mass.* (Boston: Alfred Mudge & Son, Printers, 1886).

24. Marshall et al., *History of the Town of Rockport*, 246.

25. Harbor of Refuge Committee, *Harbor of Refuge at Sandy Bay*, Appendix No. II, 31.

26. Barbara H. Erkkila, *Hammers on Stone: A History of Cape Ann Granite* (Woolwich, ME: TBW Books, 1980), 138.

27. Erkkila, *Hammers on Stone*, 140–41.

CHAPTER 3

28. Irma Whitney, "'Motif No. 1,'" in *Artists of the Rockport Art Association*, ed. Kitty Parsons Recchia, (Rockport, MA: Rockport Art Association, 1940), 132.

29. Eleanor Jewett, "Rockport Harbor, 'Motive No. 1' of American Art Is Depicted in Parade. Fish House Inspires Many a Painter," *Chicago Daily Tribune*, October 8, 1933.

30. "Painters' Fish House Begins to Rise Again," *New York Times*, July 29, 1978.

31. "Plan representing the proposed extension of the wharf of Walter W. and C.F. Wonson in the harbor of Gloucester, Mass.," by John Weber, October 1883, Salem Registry of Deeds.

32. Obituary, "Walter Wonson. License Commissioner Passed Away Early This Morning," *Gloucester Daily Times*, April 22, 1901.

33. Rick Doyle, "Motif's History Recalled," *Gloucester Daily Times*, May 26, 1984. The references to this article throughout this section are obvious in the context of the text, so I will refrain from repetitive citations where possible.

34. Obituary, "George L. Poland Dies in Rockport," *Gloucester Daily Times*, April 18, 1955.

35. Roger Martin, *Rockport Remembered: An Oral History* (Gloucester, MA: Curious Traveller Press, 1977), 37.

36. Obituary, "Capt. George H. Tarr Dies on Board His Craft," *Gloucester Daily Times*, August 13, 1919.

37. Obituary, "John R. Tarr Was Well Known Citizen," *Gloucester Daily Times*, January 23, 1924.

38. From the collection of the Cape Ann Museum.

39. Martin, *Rockport Remembered*, 64.

40. "Regulations of the Sandy Bay Pier Company, Rockport, Mass.," printed at the Review Printery, 1906. From the files of the Sandy Bay Historical Society.

41. From the log of minutes of the Sandy Bay Pier Company, Sandy Bay Historical Society.

42. Obituary, "Death of Ex-Representative James W. Bradley," *Gloucester Daily Times*, January 1, 1912.

43. Edgar J. Driscoll Jr., "Rockport Dons Gay Nineties Garb to Mark Motif No. 1 Day Founding," *Boston Daily Globe*, May 30, 1954.

44. Don Guy, "Rockport Does One-Side Job on 'Motif': Most Famous Shack Gets Coat of Paint," *Boston Daily Globe*, May 18, 1959.

45. Charles Boardman Hawes, *Gloucester by Land and Sea: The Story of a New England Seacoast Town* (Boston: Little, Brown, and Company, 1923), 112.

46. Obituary, "Capt. Sven Hanson Died Yesterday. Well Known Fish Man Long in Business at Bearskin Neck," *Gloucester Daily Times*, May 23, 1927.

47. "Cape Ann Not Downhearted, Fog or No Fog: Rockport's New Fish Freezing Plant, Built by George W. Perkins—Quarries Still Busy—A Town That Has Capitalized Her Handicaps," *Boston Herald*, July 8, 1918.

48. "Fire Destroys Rockport Cold Storage Plant. Big Structure of Interstate Fish Corporation Practically Total Loss," *Gloucester Daily Times*, August 3, 1923, 1, 8.

49. Deed of sale dated November 20, 1923, Southern Essex District Registry of Deeds, Book 2581, 33. Deeds for all the real estate transactions documented in this section can likewise be found at the Registry of Deeds for the Southern Essex District, Salem, MA.

50. Handwritten document, in the files of the Sandy Bay Historical Society.

51. Martin, *Rockport Remembered*, 127.

52. The *Rockport Review* of January 15, 1887, reported: "The Rockport Granite Co.'s scow was towed into the dock back of our office the first of the week, and now lays at Bradley's Wharf where the vessel repairing has been done the past year."

CHAPTER 4

53. Henry C. Leonard, *Pigeon Cove and Vicinity* (Boston: F.A. Searle, 1873).

54. George Willis Solley, *Alluring Rockport: An Unspoiled New England Town on Cape Ann* (Manchester-by-the-Sea, MA: North Shore Press, Inc., Printers, 1924); Arthur P. Morley, *Rockport: A Town of the Sea* (Cambridge, MA: Murray Printing Company, 1924).

55. Robert C. Carter, *A Summer Cruise on the Coast of New England* (Boston: Crosby and Nichols, 1864), 113.

56. Charles Rosebault, "Art Invades Arcadia," *New York Times*, November 5, 1922.

57. Harrison Cady, "Art Comes to Cape Ann," in *Artists of the Rockport Art Association*, 7.

58. Eleanor C. Parsons, ed., *O Rare Harrison Cady: The Life of Harrison Cady as Told to Journalist John L. Cooley* (Rockport, MA: Sandy Bay Historical Society, 2005), 86.

59. James F. O'Gorman, "Parnassus on Ledge Road: The Life and Times of East Gloucester's Gallery-on-the-Moors, 1916–1922," in *This Other Gloucester: Occasional Papers on the Arts of Cape Ann Massachusetts* (Boston: self-published, 1976), 78–82.

60. "Beauty of Rockport Attracting Artists: Permanent Art Colony Is Growing in the Old Fishing Village," *Boston Sunday Herald*, August 15, 1920.

61. W. Lester Stevens, "Cape Ann—An Artists' Paradise," *North Shore Breeze and Reminder*, April 29, 1921, 17–19.

62. Marguerite S. Shaffer, *See America First: Tourism and National Identity, 1880–1940* (Washington, D.C., and London: Smithsonian Institution Press, 2001), 137, 161.

63. Cooley, *Rockport Sketchbook*, 25.

64. "Rockport Artists Formed Association," *Gloucester Daily Times*, July 25, 1921.

65. "Permanent Art Gallery Likely. Building Fund Will Probably Be Started Soon—Art Exhibit Opens Tomorrow," *Gloucester Daily Times*, August 15, 1922.

66. A.J. Philpott, "Rockport Proves an Artist's Paradise and Haven of Rest. Art Association Has Grown Rapidly Through the Enthusiasm of Its Members—Present Exhibition Is Remarkable," *Boston Globe*, August 23, 1930.

67. "Rockport's First Show in Gallery in New Home," *Boston Sunday Post*, July 13, 1930.

68. "Art Exhibit a Great Attraction. List of Pictures Shown with Names of Contributing Artists," *Gloucester Daily Times*, August 17, 1923.

69. "Artists' Exhibit Opened Saturday. Nearly 100 Subjects Being Shown—Catholics Held Successful Lawn Fete," *Gloucester Daily Times*, August 18, 1924.

70. John L. Cooley, *A.T. Hibbard, N.A.: Artist in Two Worlds. Second Edition* (Rockport, MA: Rockport Art Association, 1996), 112–13.

71. "The Rockport Art Association. First Exhibition Shows Interesting Group of Paintings," *Gloucester Daily Times*, August 20, 1921.

72. "Rockport Association Holding Annual Exhibit," *Gloucester Daily Times*, August 7, 1928.

73. Dictionary.com. dictionary.reference.com/browse/motif.

74. Dictionary.com. dictionary.reference.com/browse/motive.
75. "Rockport Studios to Again Open Doors to the Public," *Gloucester Daily Times*, August 8, 1931; "'Low Jinks' at Art Gallery Drew Large Audience," *Gloucester Daily Times*, August 14, 1931.
76. A.J. Philpott, "Spirit of Recovery Act Permeates Artists Exhibiting at Rockport," *Boston Sunday Globe*, August 20, 1933.
77. Federal Writers' Project of the Works Progress Administration for Massachusetts, *Massachusetts: A Guide to Its Places and People* (Boston: Houghton Mifflin, 1937), 241.
78. A.J. Philpott, "Two Art Exhibitions at Rockport Full of Variety. Several Well-Known Artists Have Pictures in Association Display—Work of Ex-Soldier Students Among Features in Other," *Boston Globe*, September 1, 1922.
79. A.J. Philpott, "Booth Tarkington, Art Patron. Vose Honors Novelist as Lover of Beauty," *Boston Sunday Globe*, September 1, 1946.
80. A.J. Philpott, "Art Center of America: A Series Showing Why New England Makes This Claim in Summer Months," *Boston Globe*, July 28, 1938.

CHAPTER 5

81. "Rockport Float Wins First Prize," *Patchwork* (November–December 1933), from the Aldro T. Hibbard papers, 1914–72, *Archives of American Art*, Smithsonian Institution [reel 373].
82. "Honor Committee and Workers at Testimonial Banquet," *Gloucester Daily Times*, October 19, 1933.
83. Lewis R. Poole, "From Official Log of the Rockport Legion Float," *Gloucester Daily Times*, October 17, 1933.
84. From a May 4, 1963 letter from Somerville mayor John J. Murphy to Aldro Hibbard, from the Aldro T. Hibbard papers, 1914–72, *Archives of American Art*, Smithsonian Institution [reel 373].
85. From a notice in the *Rockport Daily News* section of the *Gloucester Daily Times*, September 25, 1933: "The finance committee of the American Legion Publicity Float wish to express appreciation to everyone who contributed to its success. Such wonderful cooperation will never be forgotten. Earl F. Greene, Chairman, A. Carl Butman, Treasurer."
86. "Rockport's Exhibit Given Sendoff to World's Fair," *Boston American*, September 25, 1933.

87. "Rockport Legion Float Headed to Buffalo," *Gloucester Daily Times*, September 27, 1933.

88. "Legion Float Left Chicago Yesterday on Homeward Trip," *Gloucester Daily Times*, October 5, 1933.

89. John Cooley, "Smiling Jimmy Quinn, a small town police officer, who..." *North Shore '74* (Weekend Magazine Supplement of Essex County Newspapers, Inc.), February 16, 1974, 8ff.

90. "Rockport Legion Float Runs into Plenty of Fog," *Gloucester Daily Times*, September 26, 1933.

91. "Legion Float Arrives in Rainstorm at Auburn, N.Y.," *Gloucester Daily Times*, September 28, 1933.

92. "Legion Float Stopped at Erie Last Evening," *Gloucester Daily Times*, September 29, 1933.

93. "Chicago Throngs Cheer March of Vets. Legion Parade Sweeps on Till Fall of Night," *Chicago Daily Tribune*, October 4, 1933.

94. "Chicago Hosts Cheer Bay State Veterans in Big Legion Parade," *Boston Herald*, October 4, 1933. The *Christian Science Monitor* of October 3, 1933, put the number at 120,000.

95. "Crew of Float Tell Story of Chicago Trip," *Gloucester Daily Times*, October 10, 1933.

96. "Model of Famed Art Site Made for Rockport Legion. Float Depicting 'Motive No. 1' Will Be Sent by Post to Chicago Convention," *Boston Globe*, September 23, 1933.

97. James O'Donnell Bennett, "Chicago Throngs Cheer March of Vets: Legion Parade Sweeps on Till Fall of Night: Thousands See Epic of Empire Pass," *Chicago Daily Tribune*, October 4, 1933.

98. Ibid.

99. "Chicago Streets Rumble to Tread of Legion's Host. 120,000 Men March All Day Acclaimed by Plaudits of Multitude," *Christian Science Monitor*, October 3, 1933.

100. "Crew of Float Tell Story of Chicago Trip," *Gloucester Daily Times*, October 10, 1933.

101. "Best Paraders of the Legion Are Announced. Drum Corps and Bands to Compete Today," *Chicago Daily Tribune*, October 4, 1933.

102. "Chicago Hosts Cheer Bay State Veterans in Big Legion Parade. 9000 Marchers, Led by Lt. Gov. Bacon, Prove Largest Visiting Contingent," *Boston Herald*, October 4, 1933.

103. "Rockport Legion Float Wins High Acclaim at Fair. Awarded First Place Among Exhibits in Mammoth Convention Parade Held at Chicago Yesterday," *Gloucester Daily Times*, October 4, 1933.

104. "Crew of Float Tell Story of Chicago Trip," *Gloucester Daily Times*, October 10, 1933.

105. "'Motif Number One' Is Back from Chicago," *Gloucester Daily Times*, October 9, 1933.

106. "Triumphant Float Given Warm Reception by Townsfolks," *Gloucester Daily Times*, October 10, 1933.

107. Cooley, *Rockport Sketchbook*, 106. In any case, the *Gloucester Daily Times* offered no specific crowd estimates on the day of the event, and this number may be part lore, recorded nearly thirty years after the event.

108. "Cape Ann Fishing Village Put Tang of Sea into Prize Float. Rugged Scene, Designed by Aldro Hibbard, Sailed Across Western Plains and Back; Displayed in Boston after Great Homecoming," *Christian Science Monitor*, October 26, 1933.

109. "Chicago Streets Rumble to Tread of Legion's Host. 120,000 Men March All Day Acclaimed by Plaudits of Multitude," *Christian Science Monitor*, October 3, 1933.

110. "Crew of Float Tell Story of Chicago Trip," *Gloucester Daily Times*, October 10, 1933.

111. "Legion Parade Trophy on Exhibition in Local Store," *Gloucester Daily Times*, October 11, 1933.

112. "Honor Committee and Workers at Testimonial Banquet," *Gloucester Daily Times*, October 19, 1933.

113. Notes of Harold Cooney, adjutant, Edward Peterson Post #98, from the files of the Sandy Bay Historical Society.

114. "Honor Committee and Workers at Testimonial Banquet," *Gloucester Daily Times*, October 19, 1933.

115. Merikay Walvogen and Barbara Brackman, *Patchwork Souvenirs of the 1933 World's Fair* (Nashville, TN: Rutledge Hill Press, 1933), 3.

116. Ibid., 13.

117. From the commemorative booklet: "Designed by the artist Aldro T. Hibbard whose supreme motive was the artistic portrayal of nature and human life unchanged by time, the 'Rockport Wharf' is not only a memory but a reality which harks back to days when men fought for life and livelihood."

CHAPTER 6

118. *Artgum* 1, no. 7 (June 1923): 10, from the collection of the Massachusetts College of Art and Design.

119. Both of these brochures are from the Aldro T. Hibbard papers, 1914–72, *Archives of American Art*, Smithsonian Institution [reel 373].

120. "'Low Jinks' at Art Gallery Drew Large Audience," *Gloucester Daily Times*, August 4, 1931.

121. Paul F. Kneeland, "'Why Shouldn't Art Pay?' Demands Anthony Thieme. He Has Painted Rockport's Motif No. 1 So Often They Call It His 'Gold Mine,'" *Boston Daily Globe*, July 26, 1945.

122. Samuel T. Williamson, "Cape Ann: Blue-Water Fishermen and Artists Give It a Deep Rooted Individuality," *Holiday Magazine* 5, no 5 (May 1949): 98 ff.

123. Obituary, "Artist Anthony Thieme Dead," *Gloucester Daily Times*, December 8, 1954.

124. Obituary, "Artist, 66, Takes His Life at Hotel," *New York Times*, December 8, 1954.

125. *Artists of the Rockport Art Association*, A3.

126. A.J. Philpott, "Anthony Thieme's Unique Art Gallery, Attracting Throngs, Talk of Cape Ann," *Boston Sunday Globe*, August 31, 1941.

127. "Famous Art Gallery Burns at Rockport," *Boston Daily Globe*, December 24, 1946.

128. Obituary, "Artist Anthony Thieme Dead," *Gloucester Daily Times*, December 8, 1954.

129. From the Rockport Board of Public Welfare meeting minutes, August 30, 1937.

130. A.J. Philpott, "Spirit of Recovery Act Permeates Artists Exhibiting at Rockport," *Boston Sunday Globe*, August 20, 1933.

131. Edward Alden Jewell, "Cape Ann's Thriving Art Industry. The Exuberant Summer Season Mounts to a Climax with the Opening of the Annual North Shore Carnival Tuesday," *New York Times*, August 23, 1936.

132. A.J. Philpott, "Colorful Paintings Shown in Rockport Art Exhibit. Men from All Walks of Life Attracted to Art Association Show Opening," *Boston Globe*, August 4, 1936.

133. "Rockport Art Galleries Hit by 'Blue' Laws," *Gloucester Daily Times*, July 12, 1937; "Chief to Seek Court Complaints Today," *Gloucester Daily Times*, July 13, 1937; "Will Defy Rockport 'Blue Law.' Artists Say They Will Exhibit on Sundays; Won't, Say Police," *Boston Sunday Post*, July 11, 1937.

134. "Seven Summoned for Keeping Open on Lord's Day," *Gloucester Daily Times*, July 14, 1937; "Bear Skin Neck Merchants Make Protest to Board," *Gloucester Daily Times*, July 16, 1937; "Claim Action of Selectmen Against Town's Interest," *Gloucester Daily Times*, July 17, 1937.

135. Lawrence Dame, "Sunday Laws Leave Rockport Drab; Town Fears Exodus of Art Colony," *Boston Herald*, July 19, 1937.

136. A.J. Philpott, "Enforcement of Blue Law Starts Rockport Commotion; Indignant Citizens Fear Death Knell for Summer Resort If Selectman Is Upheld," *Boston Sunday Globe*, July 18, 1937.

137. Lawrence Dame, "Court Upholds Rockport Ban," *Boston Herald*, July 22, 1937; *New York Times*, "Art Colony Aghast at 'Blue Law' Curb," July 25, 1937.

138. "Superior Judge Rules in Favor of Artists. Two Motions of Counsel in Famous Rockport Sunday Law Cases Allowed, Reversing Verdict of Lower Court," *Gloucester Daily Times*, October 29, 1937.

139. Robert Y. Ellis, "Blue Laws Close Rockport Art Shops," *Christian Science Monitor*, June 12, 1961; "Revised Mass. Blue Laws in Effect Today," *Boston Globe*, November 12, 1962.

140. Aldro T. Hibbard, "Leading Artist Tells of Past Two Decades Here: Stresses Importance of Holding Cape Ann's Beauty and Charm," *Cape Ann Log* 1, no. 4 (July 7, 1939), from the Aldro T. Hibbard papers, 1914–72, *Archives of American Art*, Smithsonian Institution [reel 374].

141. A.J. Philpott, "Art Center of America: Rockport Has a Charm All Its Own That Beauty Lovers Appreciate," *Boston Globe*, July 28, 1938.

142. "Prizes Offered to Art Amateurs," *Cape Ann Log* 1, no. 4 (July 7, 1939), from the Aldro T. Hibbard papers, 1914–72, *Archives of American Art*, Smithsonian Institution [reel 374].

Chapter 7

143. Katherine Woods, "The Place and the People That Are Provincetown," *New York Times*, July 12, 1942.

144. "Provincetown Opinion Split over Rockport Scene on Book," *Cape Cod Standard Times*, July 18, 1942.

145. Obituary, "Mary Heaton Vorse, a Novelist and Champion of Labor, Dead," *New York Times*, June 15, 1966.

146. Mary Heaton Vorse, *Time and the Town: A Provincetown Chronicle* (New York: Dial Press, 1942), 110–26.

147. "The Literary Life," *Time* 40, no. 9, August 31, 1942.

148. "Rockport Stirred—Motif No. 1 Is on Provincetown Book," *Boston Daily Globe*, July 18, 1942.

149. Cooley, *A. T. Hibbard*, 115.

150. Ibid., 114.

151. A.J. Philpott, "Exhibition at Rockport 2nd Most Important on North Shore This Year," *Boston Sunday Globe*, July 11, 1943.

152. Cooley, *A. T. Hibbard*, 129.

153. "Vander Meer, Red's Twirler, Takes First Lesson in Art," *Boston Globe*, June 2, 1939,

154. Al Hirshberg, "Aldro Hibbard Has His Nerve: Rockport Artist Worried About His Ball Club, Now That Navy Has Taken First Base Star," undated clipping in the Aldro T. Hibbard papers, 1914–72, *Archives of American Art*, Smithsonian Institution [reel 373].

155. "Fish Shack Faux Pas Leaves Provincetown Folk Nonplussed," *Boston Herald*, July 18, 1942.

156. "Provincetown Opinion Split over Rockport Scene on Book," *Cape Cod Standard Times*, July 18, 1942.

157. "Fish Shack Faux Pas Leaves Provincetown Folk Nonplussed," *Boston Herald*, July 18, 1942.

158. "Rockport Fish Shack 'Lifted': Selectmen Protest to Book Publishers," *Boston Herald*, July 17, 1942.

159. "Rockport Stirred—Motif No. 1 Is on Provincetown Book," *Boston Daily Globe*, July 18, 1942.

160. "Irate Rockport Commandos Set for Provincetown Raid," *Boston Herald*, July 21,1942.

161. "Rockport Artist 'Invades' Provincetown, Draws Cover for New Book on Town," *Boston Herald*, July 22, 1942.

162. "Artist Paints Cape Wharf: Commission Given to Rockport Man," *Cape Cod Standard Times*, July 22, 1942.

163. "Rockport Commando Brave Chill to Take Provincetown Objective," *Boston Herald*, July 23, 1942.

164. "Rockport Artist 'Invades' Provincetown, Draws Cover for New Book on Town," *Boston Herald*, July 22, 1942.

165. "Picture-Taking Not Banned in Provincetown Except Waterfront Scenes," *Provincetown Advocate*, July 23, 1942.

166. "'Don't Get Caught with Paints Down!' Rockport Artists Told: Gloucester Painter Ridicules Book Jacket Furore; Sees Artists' Sahara There," *Boston Traveler*, August 6, 1942.

167. "Marine Painter's Bombshell Like Cap Pistol to Rockport," *Boston Traveler*, August 7, 1942.

Chapter 8

168. "40 Artists Give Fish Shed at Rockport Coat of Paint," *Boston Daily Globe*, August 28, 1942.

169. Don Guy, "Rockport Does One-Side Job on 'Motif': Most Famous Shack Gets Coat of Paint," *Boston Globe*, May 18, 1959.

170. Cooley, *A. T. Hibbard*, 115.

171. Ralph Pearson, "Inside North Shore," unidentified clipping dated May 23, 1963, from the *Boston Herald* Newspaper Morgue, Beebe Communications Library, Boston University; John Allan Long, "To Change the Subject: Fresh Face for Motif No. 1," unidentified clipping dated June 29, 1963, from the *Boston Herald* Newspaper Morgue, Beebe Communications Library, Boston University.

172. Peter Anderson, "Motif No. 1 to Be Repainted: The Right Color Is Important," *Boston Globe*, December 1, 1976.

Chapter 9

173. A.J. Philpott, "Artists, Like Fisherman, Are Busy on Cape Ann. All Feel They Are Close to War, but Have No Fear," *Boston Sunday Globe*, August 23, 1942.

174. "Many People Gathered at Motif No. 1 Dedication. Ceremony Held Yesterday for Famous 'Symbol of Rockport'—Bronze Placque [*sic*] Unveiled," *Gloucester Daily Times*, May 15, 1950.

175. "Rockport Puts Zoning On Ballot. Voters Bought Motif-Wharf for $3600; Building Code to 1946 Election," *Gloucester Daily Times*, March 7, 1945; "Rockport Votes $3600 to Buy 77-Year-Old Fishing Shack for a War Memorial," *Gloucester Daily Times*, March 8, 1945.

176. "Noted Rockport Fish Shack to Be War Hero Memorial," *Boston Traveler*, March 7, 1945.

177. From the Board of Selectmen Records, April 5, 1945, Rockport Town Hall.

178. From the Board of Selectmen Records, October 25, 1945, Rockport Town Hall.

179. From the Board of Selectmen Records, November 1 and 23, 1945, and March 15, 1945, Rockport Town Hall.

180. From the Board of Selectmen Records, March 28 and June 13, 1946, Rockport Town Hall.

181. From the Board of Selectmen Records, February 13, 1947, Rockport Town Hall.

182. Martin, *Rockport Remembered*, 149.

183. Letter from Nicola A. Barletta, chairman of the selectmen, to G. Homer Orne, L. Dana Vibert, Dana Woods and Gene Lesch, dated April 1, 1974, in the files of the Sandy Bay Historical Society.

184. "Many People Gathered at Motif No. 1 Dedication," *Gloucester Daily Times*, May 15, 1950.

185. "Artists Duel Fishermen to Retain 'Motif,'" *Boston Globe*, April 28, 1950.

186. "Rockport Artists Up in Arms Over Wires," unattributed clipping dated April 28, 1950, from the Aldro T. Hibbard papers, 1914–72, *Archives of American Art*, Smithsonian Institution [reel 374].

187. "Artists Bury Controversy in Rockport," *Christian Science Monitor*, May 23, 1951.

188. "Rockport Perking Up for Motif No. 1 Day," *Gloucester Daily Times*, May 24, 1951.

189. "Pageantry, Ceremony Mark Motif No. 1 Day," *Gloucester Daily Times*, March 28, 1951.

190. Edgar J. Driscoll Jr., "Rockport Dons Gay Nineties Garb to Mark Motif No. 1 Day Founding," *Boston Globe*, May 30, 1954.

191. "Gloucester Bridge Nears Finish; Residents Happy," *Boston Daily Globe*, August 22, 1950.

192. Emilie Tavel, "Shack Weathers Another Storm: Watchdogs Save 'Motif No. 1' List," *Christian Science Monitor*, May 17, 1958; John Fenton, "Rockport Saves Its Classic Fishing Shanty," *New York Times*, June 8, 1958.

193. "Walt Dated World," maintained by Mouseketeer Alison, waltdatedworld.bravepages.com/id87.htm.

194. "A Nomenclature Narrative History of Circle-Vision," blog posting by Progressland, October 14, 2008, disneylandcompendium.blogspot.com/2008/10/nomenclature-narrative-history-of.html.

195. Michael Knight, "Rockport, Mass., Plans to Rebuild Coast Landmark Razed by Storm," *New York Times*, February 11, 1978.

196. Timothy Crouse, "Artists, Tourists, Agree on Rockport," *Gloucester Daily Times*, July 3, 1964.

197. Jo Bower, "Motif's Remains Come Down Piece by Piece," *Gloucester Daily Times*, February 14, 1978.

198. "Snow, Wind, Surf Batter Cape Ann," *Gloucester Daily Times*, February 7, 1978.

199. Michael Knight, "Rockport, Mass., Plans to Rebuild Coast Landmark Razed by Storm," *New York Times*, February 11, 1978.

200. Josh Odell, "Rockport Weathered the Storm—Just Barely," *Gloucester Daily Times*, February 6, 2003.

201. Nick Grabbe, "The Planning for Motif 1A," *Boston Globe*, February 19, 1978.

202. "Rockport Shore Damage in Millions," *Gloucester Daily Times*, February 8, 1978.

203. Jo Bower, "Motif's Remains Come Down Piece by Piece," *Gloucester Daily Times*, February 14, 1978.

204. "Rockport Shore Damage in Millions," *Gloucester Daily Times*, February 8, 1978.

205. Jo Bower, "Most Miss Motif, Want It to Be Rebuilt," *Gloucester Daily Times*, February 23, 1978.

206. "New Motif Accepted," *Gloucester Daily Times*, November 27, 1978.

Chapter 10

207. Donna Brown, *Inventing New England: Regional Tourism in the Nineteenth Century* (Washington, D.C., and London: Smithsonian Institution Press, 1995), 215.

208. Richard H. Love, *Carl W. Peters: American Scene Painter from Rochester to Rockport* (Rochester, NY: University of Rochester Press, 1999), 516.

209. Brown, *Inventing New England*, 205.

About the Author

L.M. Vincent has published both fiction and nonfiction, and two of his plays have been produced regionally and Off-Off Broadway. He lives north of Boston.

© copyright 2011 Robert M. Ring.

Visit us at
www.historypress.net